How to Plan Special Events and Raise Money in Early Childhood Programs

by Judith Anne Rice

Illustrations ©1997 John Bush, Minneapolis, Minnesota.

Book design by Fruitful Results, St. Paul, Minnesota.

Published by: Redleaf Press
                 a division of Resources for Child Caring
                 450 North Syndicate, Suite 5
                 St. Paul, MN 55104-4125

Distributed by: Gryphon House
                 Mailing address:
                 P.O. Box 207
                 Beltsville, MD 20704-0207

Library of Congress Cataloging-in-Publication Data

Rice, Judith, 1953–
    Let's party : how to plan special events and raise money in early
childhood programs / by Judith Anne Rice.
        p.   cm.
    ISBN 1-884834-41-8
    1. Entertaining--Planning--Handbooks, manuals, etc. 2. Children's
parties--Planning--Handbooks, manuals, etc. 3. Educational fund
raising--Handbooks, manuals, etc. 4. Early childhood education--
Finance--Handbooks, manuals, etc.
GV1472.R453   1997
790'.06'94--dc21   97-34166
                                                           CIP

Thank-you to Velma Lehman-Fox
who taught me how to plan a special event.
Her commitment to the field of early childhood
family education continues to inspire.

CONTENTS

As from the house your mother sees
You playing round the garden trees,
So you may see, if you but look
Through the windows of this book.
Mother-child, far, far away
And in another garden, play.
But do not think you can at all,
By knocking on the window call
That child to hear you. He intent
Is still on his play-business bent.
He does not hear, he will not look,
Nor yet be lured out of this book.
For long ago, the truth to say,
He has grown up and gone away.
And it is but a child of air
That lingers in the garden there.

—R. L. STEVENSON

*From the plaque in the shelter at the small park,
which we called The Duck Pond, where I played as a child.*

INTRODUCTION

I started planning events at about the age of ten, when my mother put me in charge of my two youngest brothers at naptime. To make it fun and interesting, I would start out by telling stories, giving them projects to do, and dressing up my other younger brother in a makeshift costume. He became the very reluctant "special visitor" who was always the highlight to an otherwise boring and required naptime.

For the past thirteen years I have been an early childhood teacher at The Early Childhood Family Education Program in St. Paul, Minnesota. This unique program offers weekly classes that parents and their children (from birth to five years old) attend together. Classes begin with a circle time of songs, finger plays, and dancing. We then describe the activities that have been set up for them. "Interaction time" begins when the parents and children play together and engage in developmentally appropriate activities. After thirty minutes, the children and parents separate into classes that offer support and information for the parents and a preschool experience for the children. It is a marvelous program because it empowers not only the children but also the children's most important teachers—their parents. We hope to see it continue to grow and be adopted in more states.

Special events are valuable because they provide unique opportunities for parents, children, teachers, and organizations to connect with one another in ways that strengthen individuals and communities. Providing experiences for families to "play" together helps them "stay" together. Each activity is designed to provide an educational experience to the children while they have fun.

When our early childhood program was getting started, we needed to inform people about who we were and what we were doing. Special events proved to be one of our most effective tools for doing that, and they can do the same for you.

This book draws on my experience gained through staging scores of special events. Since our lives tend to evolve around nature, the book is divided seasonally. Although the book is written with early childhood programs in mind (such as nursery schools, child care centers, family education and after-school programs), anyone who is planning a special event for young children (even naptime) will find it useful.

Remember that you are helping to create precious and everlasting memories for children and their families. Good luck and have fun!

PLANNING

Begin your planning at least a couple of months ahead of time. If you have a parent advisory board, it may want to do the majority of the planning. If you don't have a board, ask parents and others to volunteer. At a minimum, you will need to choose a theme, figure out how much money you have to spend, decide on a date and time, and determine what outside contributions might be available and what materials will be needed for activities, decorating, entertainment, food, and beverages.

Put someone in charge of soliciting support from the community. Approach businesses for donations of food or door prizes. Phone calls and letters need to be sent out as early as possible in order to avoid such last minute surprises as having either too little or too much of certain materials. The person responsible for solicitation could also be responsible for sending post-event thank-you letters to volunteers, businesses, or others who have made contributions. Be sure to thank each of them individually and make it as personal as possible, perhaps by including some of the children's artwork or some photos from the event.

Preregistration is helpful because it provides an estimate of the number of people you will be serving. Assign people to different areas, such as food or entertainment, but make sure that everyone is included in any major decisions. You will need people to help set up, supervise, and assist with the activities. After the event is over, you will need people to help take down and clean up.

The reproducible forms and patterns at the back of the book will save you time and energy in preparing some materials for the events.

ORGANIZATION Use the Special Event Organizer on page 76 to guide the planning of your event. If your organization is large and has a lot of "people power," the organizer will help you clarify who is responsible for each task. Even if you are a one-person child care provider who wants to put on an event for families, the organizer is a great checklist for making sure that you have covered all the bases. Simply delete areas that do not apply.

SCHEDULING My experience is that one and a half hours is about the right length of time for the whole event. More time than that is too long for young children, and less time does not allow for busy parents to attend at least part of the party.

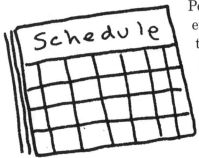

Post a schedule near the entrance of the event. This will enable participants to know what to expect and to make the best use of their time. Also display a list of contributors, or post a thank-you to each provider near the items donated.

The following page contains a sample schedule with notes on each section.

YABA-DABA-DOO
WELCOME TO THE DINO DIG PARTY!

FREE CHOICE
6:30 - 7:00 p.m.
Archeological Dino Dig
Bowling for Dinosaurs
Guess My Name
Matching Dinosaurs
Paleontologist Playground
Building with Boulders
Dino Photo-Op

[The children can choose from a variety of games, art activities, and play. Allow at least thirty minutes for Free Choice.]

LARGE GROUP
7:00 - 7:30 p.m.
Announcements, Acknowledgments, Door Prizes
Dancing to taped music: Dinosaur Rock
Singing favorite songs

[Use this time for such things as singing songs, finger plays, music, a very short video, storytelling, live entertainment, dancing, speakers, giving away door prizes, and thanking volunteers. Allow twenty to thirty minutes.]

FOOD AND BEVERAGES
7:30 - 7:55 p.m.
Prehistoric Punch
Cretaceous Cookies

[It is best to serve refreshments at the end of the event so that children do not wander around with food during the activities. This is also a good time for a volunteer in costume to mingle. There may be a waiting line for the snacks, and the time will be less trying if a dinosaur stops to talk to children while they are waiting. Free choice can be resumed at this time for children who came late or for other children who desire additional time. Allow twenty-five minutes for a juice and cookies snack. More time will be needed if you are serving a brunch or a meal.]

ANNOUNCEMENT
7:55 p.m.
The Dino Dig will end in five minutes.
Thank you for coming.

[Five minutes before the scheduled ending time, announce that the event will be over in five minutes and thank everyone for coming. That warning will help smooth the transition of leaving, which is useful to young children who may be deeply involved in projects.]

ANNOUNCEMENT
8:00 p.m.
The Dino Dig has now ended.
Thank-you for coming.
Please drive carefully.

[Five minutes later, announce that the event has just ended, thank everyone again for coming, and ask them to please drive carefully.]

FUNDRAISING   Funding seems to be an ever present need when it comes to young children. My first experience raising funds came when I was just out of college and hired to be the lead instructor at an extended day program. The parent advisory board decided it wanted to purchase some new equipment. Since we had exactly zero dollars in our account, the question arose, "How does one squeeze blood out of a turnip?" We decided to ask parents and people in the community to clean out their garages and to donate their "treasures" to our sale. We raised $232. This may not seem impressive, but I was extremely pleased because we started with no money and generated those dollars in a community that was economically depressed.

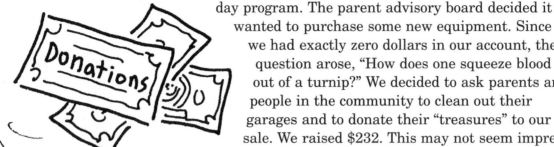

Here are some other ways to raise funds:

- Put together an audiotape of the children singing their favorite songs. You could also include a few solos by talented adults in your group. Make inexpensive copies and sell them.

- Sell calendars that are made up of children's artwork.

- Host an ice cream social.

- Sell cookbooks compiled from favorite family recipes.

- If you know several people who would be willing to donate a lot of time and are very good on the computer, they could put together a cookbook and artwork made by the children to sell and publicize your program. As an alternative, use one of the many companies who specialize in putting the book together for you. For a free packet of samples and information, call Walter's Publishing (1-800-447-327). To get the discount they provide to fundraisers, ask for their Partnership Program.

- Put on a Walk-a-Thon.

- Sell seedlings on Arbor Day.

- Produce a play or talent show.

- Have a carnival.

- Stage a style show with new and secondhand clothing.

- Conduct a house and garden tour.

- Offer seminars. Invite a guest speaker on a "hot" parenting topic.

- Provide such services as babysitting, house-sitting, snow removal, or pet care.

- Hold a bake sale.

- Sell T-shirts, sweatshirts, and book bags with your logo on them.

- Sell plants and flowers.

- Set up a crafts show. Sell booth space.
- Sell raffle tickets for handmade quilts, hotel accommodations, or just about anything that people might want. Verify that raffles are legal in your community and that your organization follows any laws or ordinances that may apply. Make the raffle tickets difficult to reproduce, and require the winner to have proper identification.

You may choose to work with one of the many companies that help organizations attempting to raise funds by providing products for them to sell. Each company has its own arrangements, but generally your organization will receive a percentage or some other incentive based on sales. Make sure that the fundraising company you choose is reputable by asking these questions from the Association of Fundraisers & Direct Sellers (AFRDS):

- How long has the company (and the company's representative) been in the business?
- How, specifically, will the company help implement the program (for example, kick-off, presentation, teacher/parent letters, handling of returned merchandise)?
- How will the company tailor the program to fit your organization's particular needs or rules?
- Does the company understand and comply with your state sales tax laws, and how will these laws impact your program?
- Does the company guarantee their products?
- What is the company's policy on replacing damaged products?
- Will the company give the organization credit or buy back undeliverable or unsold goods?
- How responsive will the company be to other problems, such as incorrect or lost orders?

For a free list of AFRDS member companies operating in your state and community, write to:

Association of Fundraisers & Direct Sellers
Department L
Suite 500-G
5775 Peachtree-Dunwoody Road
Atlanta, GA 30342

PUBLIC RELATIONS Invite the press. They may not always attend, but keeping them aware of the vitality of your program may serve you well in the future. Send out a press release at least one month ahead of time, if possible, so that community newspapers will be able to include it in the appropriate issue. Try to construct paragraphs that the newspaper can use "as written."

The press release must include the basics, such as who you are, the name and purpose of the event, and where and when it will be held. Always include a contact person who can be reached for further information. As shown in the sample on the following page, the release should be written on your letterhead and should always contain the heading "FOR IMMEDIATE RELEASE" with a contact person and phone number across from it.

Including a picture with the press release, especially one containing a child, will improve the chances of it being published. For example, prior to the event, you might stage a picture of one of your children shaking the hand of a firefighter. Be creative. Having a good quality camera is a wise investment. If you do not own one, borrow one and use black-and-white film, since that is the preference of most news organizations, and it photocopies well. If you know any experienced or professional photographers, ask them to volunteer to take photographs.

Your special events will benefit from other publicity and promotions throughout the year. For example, have refrigerator magnets made with your logo and telephone number on them. Give them to people who are interested in finding out more about your program. Our program also has offered a "Pass to Class" to parents in the neighborhood. The pass entitles parents to visit one of our classes with no fee or obligation. We arranged to have a local McDonalds include the passes in its kids meals.

Set up booths at local fairs and festivals. Make sweatshirts, T-shirts, book bags, and rulers with your logo on them and sell them at cost. Volunteer to serve on councils and boards in your community. Encourage parents to be active and up-to-date on legislative issues pertinent to families and children. Get to know the people at your community and city newspapers, invite them to everything, and send them a lot of adorable pictures along with accurate and on-time press releases.

After the event, be sure to thank contributors and volunteers. To make it more personal, include photographs from the event that show the individual donations. Or you might choose one great picture to put into all of the notes. Also, posters and thank-yous made by the children are always appreciated.

Thank You
FOR HELPING TO MAKE OUR EASTSIDE E.C.F.E. MULTICULTURAL WINTER EVENT SUCH A TREMENDOUS SUCCESS!

Here is an example of a thank-you card created by a member of our advisory council.

Early Childhood Family Education
EASTSIDE
Located at: Eastside Community Center
1526 E. Sixth Street, Saint Paul, MN 55106
555-1234

FOR IMMEDIATE RELEASE

FOR ADDITIONAL INFORMATION CALL VELMA LEHMAN-FOX AT 555-1234

The Eastside Early Childhood Family Education Program, St. Paul Public Schools, is sponsoring a Family Fun and Information Fair from 10:00 a.m. to 2:00 p.m. at the Eastside Community Center, located at 1526 East Sixth Street, St. Paul, MN.

The event is aimed at families with children birth to five years and their siblings. The fair will provide access to many community resource programs, including Ramsey County Public Health, Minnesota Poison Control, St. Paul police and fire departments, Minnesota State Highway Patrol, University of Minnesota Extension Division, American Cancer Society, Resources for Child Caring, and Kaplan School Supplies.

Parents can have their children's car seats checked for proper installation and use through the Project Safe Baby program sponsored by the Midas Corporation and the Minnesota State Highway Patrol. Project Safe Baby also provides parents with car seats at wholesale cost from any of the thirty Twin Cities Midas dealers. When the car seat is no longer needed, it may be returned to a Midas shop in exchange for services equal to the amount paid for the seat.

The classrooms will be open with fun and exciting activities for young children, including a puppet show, Buckles the Bunny, and spin-art!

Community Education

INVITATIONS

Invitations are your opportunity to attract a large crowd to the event. They create the first impression in the minds of your potential guests. Whenever possible, use quality paper. Make them stand out by using strong colors. Have invitations available at your site for parents to pick up, and mail them to outsiders at least two weeks before the event. At the same time, display posters at the site and distribute flyers throughout the community. Special events are always good photo opportunities. Be sure that the invitation suggest that parents bring a camera, especially when offering activities that require taking pictures. If you have the means and prefer to develop your own invitations from scratch, the reproducible forms at the back of the book can serve as starting points. Or you may simply insert your own specific information and use them as is. Use the space after the punch line of each invitation to provide important or enticing information. For example, you might list some of the activities you have decided upon, entertainment or celebrities that will be there, door prizes, and food and beverages. This space can also be used for requests. If you are having a brunch and you need people to bring baked goods, ask for them here.

ACTIVITIES

Many of the activities in early childhood can utilize such recyclable materials as buttons, artificial flowers, fabric, wood, and construction scraps. People are happy to give up material that is collecting dust in their attics, closets, and basements, as long as it will be put to good use. Just get the word out well in advance as to what you are looking for, and you will be amazed at the response. Make sure you have plenty of supplies for each activity. During the event, the parents will be helping their children, but you still need someone stationed at each activity to explain it, replenish supplies, offer help, and assist with any disasters that may occur beyond the usual expected messes. Keep in mind that for young children it is the process, not the product, that is most important. So make sure that the children enjoy doing the activities and compliment their efforts, but don't pressure them to perform to adult standards.

ATTIRE

Some events lend themselves to having the children dressed in costumes. These should be very simple. If costumes require painting, teachers and children should prepare them ahead of time so they can be worn at the event. My experience is that most young children do not last long in full-fledged costumes, even though most parents would like them to. The children get hot, the costumes get stained, wings can get in the way, and some children will be upset because they don't have a costume. Often, simple props are preferable alternatives (hats, stick-on mustaches, headbands, vests, simple makeup). If costumes are in order, have a parade at the beginning of the party so that everyone can "show off," and then set them aside, if desired, to prevent them from interfering with the fun. Another simple alternative is to provide painted backdrops and a few simple props for the families to stand in front of and have their pictures taken. The preparation of a backdrop can be time consuming, but it is well worth it because it can be used for years to come.

DECORATIONS

Decorating is one area in which you should let your imagination roam. Use yards of sheer, inexpensive fabric and twinkly lights. Display objects in ways that are unusual, such as hanging watering cans and umbrellas from the ceiling at a baby shower. Make sure everything is secured in place and that no fire hazards are created. A lot of the decorating can be done using things the children themselves have made. You might also want to keep an eye out for department store displays that could be used for special events. Leave your name and telephone number with the store manager and ask to be called if they are willing to donate them after they are no longer needed.

ENTERTAINMENT

Many people think that anyone can entertain children, but in fact, it takes someone with a lot of experience who really understands children to do a good job. Once we hired a woman to do a puppet show for our annual family picnic. She was somewhat disheveled and scantily clad. More attention was paid to her inappropriate dress than to the puppets. Our parent advisory board, which had worked so hard to raise money to pay for the entertainment, was very disappointed. Always preview the entertainment to make sure it is right for your purposes. You, not the entertainer, will be held accountable for any failures.

Make sure that any necessary equipment is available for the entertainers. For example, you may need to provide such things as extension cords, lighting, certain seating arrangements, sound systems, or protection from the elements. If animals will be present, they may need special considerations.

When you are discussing the fees, it never hurts to ask entertainers if they offer discounts, for example, to nonprofit organizations. Or they may offer a discount to members of chains to gather future business from other chain members. Some entertainers are willing to accept a lower fee for a brief performance at a special event.

You may want to include video entertainment. Have the children view it prior to the event, or have a theater-type space set up away from the chaos. That way the video can run continuously and be seen and heard by everyone as they come and go. An exception to this would be if you are showing a video to be seen by all attendees as a group. You can obtain some great music and videos from your library and local children's specialty stores. If you have a tax exempt number, call Rounder Kids Music Distribution (1-800-223-6357) to receive a free school and library catalog. *Party Dance Favorites* (Special Music Company, 1989) and *The Ultimate Party Survival Kit* (Sony Music Entertainment, 1995) are two recordings that are useful for a range of special events because they have many favorites, like "Bunny Hop," "Limbo," "Chicken Dance," and "Hokey Pokey." It is exciting for the children to have a "celebrity" (a volunteer in costume) make an appearance. Most fabric stores have a selection of costumes and patterns that can be made for both children and adults. At our Dinosaur Dig Party, we provided a grandmother with the fabric necessary to sew us a beautiful dinosaur costume. The total cost was less than a one-time rental charge, and in addition to having it available for future events, we now lend it out to parents and other programs. We only require that it comes back clean. I strongly recommend constructing and lending costumes because it is cost effective and a fun way to build goodwill with other programs and people.

FOOD

Even though young children require small amounts of food, it can be expensive and time consuming to serve a large group. For the most part, it is best to keep the food very simple, usually something to drink and something commercially prepared to eat. For those events that require food preparation, make sure there are no rules restricting the kinds of foods that you intend to serve. For example, some programs or ordinances require that only commercially prepared foods be served or that noncommercial foods be prepared on-site. Always confirm that food handlers are following health and safety rules regarding food preparation, storage, and service.

Here are some tips:

- Don't serve anything messy.
- Avoid food and beverages that will stain.
- It is not always possible, but try to avoid foods that depend on refrigeration or heating.
- Do not serve foods that can easily lodge in the throats of children (hot dogs, grapes, celery sticks, carrot sticks, hard candy).
- Give juice boxes to toddlers instead of cups of juice.
- Have dry breakfast cereal on hand as a snack for very small children.
- Stay away from food or beverages containing honey, caffeine, or peanut butter.
- If you are serving coffee to the adults, have only decaffeinated coffee available, or serve both decaf and regular.

RENTALS   Some companies provide rental equipment for special events. Although most events do not require rental equipment, the following list gives some idea of what is available. This list is not complete, and companies' product lines vary, so check with your local supplier.

Concessions
Tropical Sno ice shaver, pretzel display, pizza ovens, fresh popcorn machines, cotton candy maker, refrigerators.

Balloons
Bulk balloons, strings, helium tanks, 12-foot advertising balloons, The Balloon Typhoon (a 12-foot inflated clown head with 50 balloons blowing around inside). I recommend using balloons only for decorating or as part of an activity. If given to children, they can create choking hazards.

Rides and Fun
These are designed for the youngest children: tub swing, auto ride, merry-go-round, ball crawl, Ferris wheel, sea of balls, Twista (self-propelled bumper cars), trackless kiddie train, Funland (a maze that includes a ball crawl, cargo net, and a slide).

Miscellaneous
Bubble machines, wishing well, croquet, gunny sacks, costumes, sand art, beanbag games, streamers, tickets, moonwalks, booths, tents. We once rented a spin-art machine, which everyone enjoyed. You can also use an old, large salad spinner: Place a paper plate at the bottom of the spinner, squirt paint onto the plate, replace the cover, and spin. If you would like to purchase your own inexpensive machine, ABC School Supply sells *Paint 'n Swirl* (1-800-669-4222).

FALL EVENTS

Family Fun and Information Fair

A fair that informs families of community resources is a great way to collaborate with other programs, agencies, and businesses. Families appreciate finding out what kinds of information, support, and resources are available to them. Your first step should be to prepare and distribute Participation Solicitation Forms. An example is shown on page 17. Contact a wide range of resources, such as:

County nurses

Parents Anonymous

Immunization health educators

Local clinics

Police department

Fire department

American Red Cross

County nutritionists

Resource programs that deal with families of young children

Businesses that sell goods related to early childhood (diaper services, preschool suppliers, kid specialty stores, or people that give lessons in music, dance, tutoring)

The following event illustrates how your program can gain both expertise and materials from collaborating with local companies who have projects aimed at young children. We contacted the Midas Corporation, who began Project Safe Baby as a reaction to a report that the leading cause of death among children is motor vehicle crashes. The program allows parents to purchase car seats at wholesale cost from any Midas shop and, when the car seat is no longer needed, return it in exchange for services equal to the amount they paid for the seat. At our Family Fun Fair, Midas worked with the state patrol to examine car seats for proper installation and use. Shockingly, over 90 percent of the car seats inspected had either been recalled by the manufacturers or weren't being used properly. Midas also gave away ten new car seats to families who could not afford new ones. Everyone received free brochures and information on how to travel more safely with children. After you have received all of the responses to your solicitations and you know who will be represented at the fair, put together a flyer listing the participants and describing the activities for the children. Circulate the flyer as widely as possible, and also let the media know about the fair. See the sample press release on page 9. On the day of the event, make sure there are enough tables or stations for all of the participants. Try to be as accommodating to participants as possible, since many of them are volunteering their time. Also make sure that each receives a personalized letter thanking them for their participation. Use the reproducible example to make invitations for this event (see page 75).

ACTIVITIES

Visiting Booths
Set up booths that are staffed by the experts you have invited. The parents can circulate throughout the fair, collecting information, talking to the expert participants, and taking time out now and then to play with their children.

Children Play Areas
Set up tables for children to play with playdough, favorite manipulatives, or paint.

DECORATIONS

Tie a helium balloon to each station.

ENTERTAINMENT

A puppet show is a big drawing card for any event. Most children are completely enamored with puppets, and so are the parents. A simple, short puppet show that repeats every 30 minutes is a real treat. Try to get some capable teenagers to be the puppeteers. Ahead of time, record an educational story along with background music. That way, all the teens have to do is manipulate the actions of the puppets. Always remind the children before the show starts that they must not touch the puppets while they are performing. Children seem to instinctively want to get up and touch them. A refrigerator box makes an excellent puppet house. Cut out a window or stage area in the front, and make a cut on the side to create a door that opens and closes. Paint the inside black and the outside any color you like. I have used these at book signings and to put on various shows at schools, libraries, and special events. They are great because they are practically free, functional, lightweight, durable, and fold up to fit inside even a small hatchback car. Invite a local celebrity such as the mayor or a person in the arts to circulate during the fair. Have volunteers dress up as favorite children's characters and mingle with the guests.

REFRESHMENTS

Serve coffee, milk, and baked goods. It has been our experience that local grocery stores and bakeries are happy to donate cookies, donuts, or muffins for events like this one.

Early Childhood Family Education
EASTSIDE
Located at: Eastside Community Center
1526 E. Sixth Street, Saint Paul, MN 55106
555-1234

June 7, 1995

The Eastside Early Childhood Family Education Program (ECFE) is sponsoring a Family Fun and Information Fair on Saturday, September 12th, from 10:00 a.m. to 2:00 p.m., for Eastside families with children from birth to 5 years and their siblings. Community resource programs are being invited to participate in providing information about their services and to send a representative to talk with parents and children who attend.

Eastside ECFE has recently relocated to 1526 East 6th Street, St. Paul, in the new Eastside Community Center connected to Harding High School.

To plan appropriately, please provide the following information indicating the willingness and commitment of your program to participate in this community-centered fair.

- -

If you are planning to participate, please detach here.
Send lower half to: Velma Lehman-Fox, 1526 E. 6th Street, St. Paul, MN 55106
Keep the upper half for your planning purposes.

Program title as it should appear for publicity
_____

Address
_____

Contact person
_____

Telephone
_____

Participating person
_____

PLEASE PROVIDE THE FOLLOWING INFORMATION

A brief description of the type of materials and/or presentation you will make:
_____
_____
_____

Resources that you will provide:
_____
_____
_____
_____

SAINT PAUL
PUBLIC SCHOOLS   LIFELONG LEARNING

Community Education

E.C.F.E.

Walk-a-Thon

Collecting donations from people who are willing to sponsor participants in an outdoor hike is a great way for nonprofit programs to generate money. A walk-a-thon also provides an opportunity for fresh air, exercise, and getting to know other parents and children. Prior to the event, our families collect donations from friends and relatives who are willing to contribute to the Parent Advisory Fund. The money is used for such things as equipment and special events. Total donations should be recorded on reproductions of the form on page 78 and turned in with the form at the walk-a-thon. Make invitations for this event from the reproducible example (see page 75). Be sure to include an alternative date and time in case of inclement weather.

ACTIVITIES

The Walk
Meet at a nearby walking path. Map out a route ahead of time that is not too far for young children. Twenty minutes seems to be about the right amount of walking. People with infants and toddlers can bring strollers or wagons, and older children might like to hitch a ride for part of the walk. It is fun to provide parents with crepe paper streamers for decorating the wagons and strollers. Start the walk as soon as a fair amount of people have arrived. Late arrivals can join in at their leisure.

Pledge Collection
Designate a person and place to collect any donations as people arrive for the event. That same person can be the contact for collecting donations after the event.

REFRESHMENTS   Provide coffee, cider, and muffins.

BOOKS

I Went Walking, by Sue Williams (San Diego: Harcourt, 1989).

Let's Go Riding In Our Strollers, by Fran Manushkin (New York: Hyperion, 1993).

Funny Walks, by Judy Hindley (Mahwah, NJ: Troll, 1994).

Field Trips

Field trips are a lot more fun when you include parents. Remind parents to keep track of their children at all times, and do head counts after any transitions. Also plan an alternate date if you are depending on nature to cooperate. Make arrangements to provide a bus or van, or have parents car pool and agree to meet at a designated time. If transportation is a problem, consider taking a neighborhood walk to a nearby park, pond, playground, construction site, or post office. Check to see if someone in the neighborhood has a garden you might tour, a house that is being renovated, or some other point of interest. Every neighborhood is dotted with people who have unusual hobbies or talents. I know a teacher who took her class to tour an artist's home that included the artist's studio. Invitations to the event can be made from the reproducible example (see page 75).

Here are some suggested destinations:

hospital
aquarium
radio station
music studio
sculpture garden
pet store
art gallery
theater
farmers market
arboretum
planetarium
garden center
berrypicking farm
apple orchard
fire station
museum
zoo
farm
library

Many of your parents may have occupations that are interesting to children and can provide a great excursion. Ask them. For example, one of our parents is a volunteer fire fighter, so he and his wife, a paramedic, arranged a great trip to the fire station.

ATTIRE	Remind people to dress appropriately. The weather was unusually cold on one of our visits to an apple orchard, and the trip was miserable because no one was dressed warmly enough.
REFRESHMENTS	Provide individual cartons of juice and baggies filled with animal crackers.
BOOKS	*Open the Door Let's Explore More*, by Rhoda Redleaf (St. Paul: Redleaf, 1996).

Fall Ball

The enjoyment of fall is intensified because it is so short-lived. Many people choose autumn as their favorite season. The crisp air, traditional foods, and the gorgeous colors found in nature are cause for celebration. Invitations can be prepared from the reproducible example (see page 75).

ACTIVITIES

Autumn Wreaths
Ahead of time, cut circles from the center of 9-inch paper plates. Provide plenty of colorful fall leaves, dried grasses, flowers, weeds, glue sticks, and autumn-colored ribbons. The children decorate their paper plates. Parents can then add a bow or a piece of ribbon for hanging the wreath.

Autumn Bookmarkers
Provide precut 8" x 9" rectangles of clear contact paper, precut 1" x 3" pieces of construction paper, markers, and a variety of fall leaves and foliage. The children should write their names on the construction paper. If necessary, parents can help to ensure the names are readable. Grasp the long edge of the backing on the contact paper and peel halfway back. Arrange the name tag and leaves on the exposed contact paper any way desired. Finally, remove the rest of the backing and fold the two halves together.

Fall Free-For-All
Cut a refrigerator box lengthwise into two halves and secure the ends with duct tape. Fill each box with about 9 inches of fall leaves. Allow two children at a time to dive, jump, and throw leaves around inside each box.

Hay Maze
Try to get someone to donate and deliver bales of hay. Form a maze for the children to navigate. You might treat them to an inexpensive and fun surprise at the exit of the maze, perhaps a couple of tulip bulbs for planting in the fall.

Pumpkin Painting
Paint pumpkins with tempera paints to which you have added a little liquid detergent. Before it dries, wash it off in preparation for the next person's turn. If the stem becomes soaked from repeated washing, it may fall off. Let the children know ahead of time that they will not be taking the pumpkin home and that someone else will paint it when they are finished. Unless you have access to an unlimited supply of pumpkins, the emphasis here is on process, not product.

Face Painting
Use Caran d'Ache Swedish Water Soluble Crayons for makeup. The colors are brilliant, won't smear, are water soluble, and the crayons will last for years. Face painting should be kept simple (a red dot on the end

of the child's nose or a few whiskers). Be sure to rinse and wipe off each crayon before you use them on another child to avoid spreading germs. Stay away from lips and eyes.

Hayrides
Children will enjoy a "mini-hayride" just as much as they would a real one. Borrow several children's wagons and fill them with hay. Weather permitting, set up a path outside, or inside if desired. Parents can give hayrides by pulling the wagons around the path.

Stuff a Scarecrow
To make a scarecrow, use an adult-sized pair of coveralls. Add slippers, a flannel shirt, gloves, and a brown grocery bag with a scarecrow face drawn on it. The head could also be a pumpkin with a face drawn on it. Have a few of the children stuff the body with real hay or crumpled up newspaper. Prop it up in a chair.

DECORATIONS Hang paper bats, bales of hay, cornstalks, pumpkins, and gourds. After the children have completed stuffing the scarecrow, display it prominently.

REFRESHMENTS Serve apple cider, pumpkin cookies, or pumpkin cupcakes. The cupcakes are made by frosting plain cupcakes with orange frosting and adding short pretzels for stems and spearmint leaf gumdrops for leaves.

BOOKS *Pumpkin, Pumpkin,* by Jeanne Titherington (New York: Scholastic, 1986).

When Autumn Comes, by Robert Maass (New York: Scholastic, 1990).

One Fall Day, by Molly Bang (New York: Geenwillow, 1994).

Ska-tat! by Kim Knutson (New York: Macmillan, 1993).

Peacemaker Gathering

Many of us feel powerless to do anything about the violence that seems to pervade our society. A peacemaker gathering gives families the opportunity to take action to create peace in their own lives and in their community. Use the reproducible example to make invitations for this event (see page 75).

ACTIVITIES

Toy Gun Buy-Back

Labeling guns and other violent objects as "toys" teaches children that they are harmless and fun. Because a child cannot distinguish between a toy gun and a real one, it is dangerous for them to play with toy guns. It is better to encourage nonviolent play and thereby help build a less violent world. For these reasons, communities are beginning to sponsor toy gun buy-backs. One such buy-back in St. Paul involved over thirty-two organizations and businesses collaborating with the Eastside Health Coalition. In exchange for the toy guns, they gave vouchers for both free admission to the Minnesota Children's Museum and free memberships in the Minnesota Parenting Association. Creative Kidstuff, a children's specialty merchandiser, also sponsored a buy-back and gave children who turned in toy guns a voucher good toward purchases from their stores. You may decide not to offer incentives at all, but to just collect toy guns and other toys that promote violence. Buy-backs sponsored by early childhood programs send an important message to parents: guns are inappropriate for children to play with.

Mad Hatter

At a table, have blank recipe cards, markers, and several old or unusual hats. This activity will help children think of constructive ways to deal with anger. The parents and their child brainstorm, trying to think of appropriate ways to handle anger. They may consider such actions as taking a time out, counting to ten, breathing deeply, or breaking Popsicle sticks. On separate recipe cards, the parents then write down each idea and place them in a hat. After contributing ideas to a hat, the children can close their eyes and select cards written by someone else. Parents and children can then discuss the suggestions on that card.

Friendship Map

Give large sheets of butcher paper and markers to several children at a time. Seat the children around the paper and have them draw a picture of where they live. Next, they take turns drawing roads, highways, and freeways from their house to the house of a friend. An adult should then label the road or highway using the name of the child who drew it. For example, "Lois Lane" or "Hannah's Highway." When all of the children have had a turn drawing a road, give them toy cars so they can "travel" from one friend's house to another.

Hug a Bug

Gather a group of children and demonstrate how to appropriately hug another person. Play fun dancing music. When the music stops, have the children find one or several other children to hug until the music resumes. Everyone then starts dancing again and the process repeats.

Feather Painting

Pass out large colorful feathers purchased at a craft store. Pair children up and ask them to sit across from one another. Tell them that they are going to take turns pretending to paint each other in a very soft, gentle way, using a feather as a brush. Explain how important it is that they do not paint too close to their partner's eyes. Guide them into painting their partner's hair, cheeks, arms, nose, under-chin, and other areas. Speak very softly and slowly. This is an extremely calming and delightful activity.

Pledge

Both parents and children fill out their own "Hands Are Not for Hitting" pledge. Use the reproducible form on page 79.

DECORATIONS Display red helium balloons.

ENTERTAINMENT Have a few individuals address the whole group, each of them sharing a brief story of peace and kindness that they performed or that someone else did for them. Arrange these speakers ahead of time, and try to get a diverse group. Don't be afraid to ask a resident of a local nursing home or the mayor. After the speakers are through, invite families to go back into the community and commit acts of peace and kindness on a daily basis.

Off to the side, continuously play the video, *The Red Balloon* (Nelson Entertainment, Films Montsouris, 1956).

REFRESHMENTS Provide flavored rice cakes, herbal teas, and juices.

BOOKS *Guess How Much I Love You*, by Sam McBratney (New York: Scholastic, 1994).

The Berenstain Bears and Too Much TV, by Stan & Jan Berenstain (New York: Random, 1984).

Make Someone Smile and 40 More Ways to Be a Peaceful Person, by Judy Lalli (Minneapolis: Free Spirit, 1996).

The Kindness Curriculum, by Judith Rice (St. Paul: Redleaf, 1995).

The Loveables in the Kingdom of Self-Esteem, by Diane Loomans (Tiburon, CT: Kramer, 1991).

Inside of Me If I Feel . . ., by Nancy Lee Walter (Minneapolis: Naturally Nan, 1993).

Everybody Has Feelings, by Charles C. Avery (Seattle: Open Hand, 1992).

Jamaica Tag-Along, by Juanita Havill (New York: Scholastic, 1989).

Book Fair

Instilling an appreciation for reading equips a child for a lifetime of learning. Decide the type of book fair you wish to stage: new or used, swaps, retailer sales, or a combination. Here are some suggestions. Solicit new and used book donations from individuals and businesses in the community. Invite attendees to bring books to be swapped for other books. Ask a local children's bookstore to sell books at the fair. If possible, arrange for them to give you a percentage of the profits. Scholastic Books can provide you with everything you need to sell new books, including posters, shelves, training videos on staging the book fair, and plenty of popular books. To identify the contact in your area, call Scholastic (1-800-724-6527). A good time to hold the book fair is during National Children's Book Week, November 18-24. Make invitations for this event from the reproducible example (see page 75).

ACTIVITIES

Bookworm Photo
Set up a photo opportunity area where children can pose as an adorable bookworm. Just roll the child's body in a green blanket, add a real graduation cap (or one made from black construction paper), and a pair of large, dark-framed glasses (lenses removed). Position the "worm" on the floor, looking at a book.

Storyteller Stage
Have someone who is fun and expressive read favorite children's books. This can be done either from a stage in a large group setting or in a quiet corner with lots of big pillows on which the children can sit comfortably.

Book Signing
Invite an author or illustrator of children's books to talk and do a book signing.

Family Collage Bookmarkers
Ask the parents to bring photographs to be cut up to make a family collage bookmarker. Provide precut 8" x 9" rectangles of clear contact paper, precut 1" x 3" pieces of construction paper, and markers. The children should write their names on the construction paper with help from parents, if necessary, to ensure readability. Grasp the long edge of the backing on the contact paper and peel halfway back. Arrange the name tag and cutup photos on the exposed contact paper any way desired. Finally, remove the rest of the backing and fold the two halves together.

Make a Book
Families can write and illustrate their very own books. Give them plenty of tagboard (for the covers), paper, pencils, crayons, markers, glue sticks, hole punches, yarn, scissors, and old magazines. Each family can be as creative as it likes in assembling cutouts and photos they have brought and in writing great prose.

The Bookworm Club

Discussing books before, during, and after reading reinforces the warm relationship connection that children associate with reading. That connection is just as important to future reading success as the actual reading! Use the reproducible form on page 80 to help the children become bookworms. Each child can paste a small photo of themselves or draw a self-portrait at the top of the form. The forms can be used either in your program or sent home to encourage family reading. After reading the child a story, fill in the book title, your own name, and some comments about the book that the child wishes to make. When the list is filled, the child can get a new form from your program. Respectfully encourage all families to participate. Children whose families choose not to participate can read with people in your program so they feel included in this project.

Make a Bookworm Puppet

You will need plenty of old socks, fabric glue, Elmer's Glitter Glue, pompoms, fabric scraps, yarn, and store-bought wiggly eyes. Let the children create their own worm puppets by gluing the scraps and glitter onto a sock. It is not necessary to cut out a mouth because that space is created well enough by the hand once it's inside the sock.

REFRESHMENTS   Provide crisp fall apples, cheese, and crackers.

Fantasy Photos

Parents love to take adorable pictures of their children. Provide a variety of backdrops and props with which the children can pose. Invite parents to bring their own camera to photograph their children in a variety of settings. For parents who do not bring a camera, have a volunteer take the pictures at each station. Borrow several Polaroid cameras, or check them out from a lending library. At the time the picture is taken, charge the parents for the cost of the film used. Gather props and costumes from parents, Goodwill stores, costume shops, and children's specialty stores. Weeks ahead of time, pass out to parents a list describing what you are looking for. Backdrops can be painted with tempera on refrigerator boxes. Invitations to the event can be made from the reproducible example (see page 75).

ACTIVITIES

Super Hero/ine
Make sure an adult is checking the child as he or she lays on top of a table wearing a red cape. Take the picture from a side view. Make the area under the table look like a city skyline so that the "Super Hero/ine" appears to be flying through the air.

Bunny Babies
Make bunny ears out of pink construction paper and attach them to a paper headband. Use face makeup to add a pink nose and whiskers. Surround the "bunny" with baskets filled with artificial flowers.

Entomologist *(an expert on insects)*
Hang a large paper butterfly from the ceiling. The children dress up as entomologists, hold a large butterfly net, and wear a safari hat (from a costume store or paper goods store).

Dress Up
Provide a lot of adult clothing, gloves, purses, hats, feather boas, and jewelry. Let the children dress themselves.

Athlete of the Year
Pose each child with a favorite piece of sports equipment, such as a football, basketball, tennis racquet, or toy golf set.

Cave Dwellers
A prehistoric snaggletooth tiger vest can be made ahead of time from a full-sized grocery bag. It is important to start with the bag properly

folded. Lay the bag flat and then fold the bottom in half so that both sides of the bag are fully exposed. Starting at the middle of one side, use a scissors to cut at an angle through the bottom and to a point that is approximately 2 inches from the opposite side. Next, open up the bag. On the uncut side, about 2 inches from the bottom of the bag, cut a hole for the arm. The bottom now forms the shoulder of the vest. Fold in the pointed section of the shoulder toward the armhole. Make the bottom edge jagged. Paint the vest to look like a cave dweller costume.

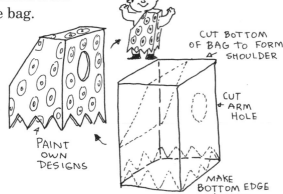

At the event, the children pose for pictures wearing the vest and holding a large bone. Paint a prehistoric backdrop with an erupting volcano (red glitter for molten lava) on a refrigerator box.

Cowpoke
The children pose for pictures wearing a cowboy hat, bandanna, and vest while riding a stick pony.

Camera Shop
Set up a dramatic play area for the children with a lot of old, empty cameras for them to pretend to take pictures of each other.

Picture Frames
Buy inexpensive precut picture frames from S&S Arts and Crafts catalog (1-800-243-9232) or cut out your own frames from tagboard paper. Decorate them with wallpaper samples from old sample books obtained from local wallpaper and paint stores. You may want to consider the following examples for making frames that match the photo:

Super Hero	*fold aluminum foil over the frame*
Bunny Babies	*glue cotton balls on the frame*
Entomologist	*use rubber stamps to print insects on the frame*
Dress Up	*decorate the frame with silk flowers*
Athlete of the Year	*make a collage frame with pictures cut from sports magazines*
Prehistoric	*glue gravel on the frame*
Cowpoke	*glue rope on the frame*

REFRESHMENTS
Serve cheese crackers and punch made by mixing a favorite fruit juice and lemon-lime soda.

BOOK
Dress Ups, by Anne Geddes (New York: Cebco, 1995).

Dinosaur Dig

Children are fascinated with dinosaurs. Instead of being terrified, children love these gigantic, ferocious creatures. Many four year olds can pronounce long difficult names and correctly identify species that have been extinct for millions of years. Because of their intense interest, this event is sure to be a success with all children. Invitations can be prepared from the reproducible example (see page 75).

(see page 75)

ACTIVITIES

Archeological Dino Dig

Ask a butcher for some very large beef bones. Scrub the bones clean and then dry them in a 200 degree oven for 30 minutes. Bury them in the sand table so that young "archeologists" can search for buried dinosaur bones! To brighten up the event, add glitter to the sand. This is an extremely popular activity.

Bowling for Dinosaurs

The children try to bowl down inflatable dinosaurs with foam boulders. So that more than one can be bowling at the same time, set up several alleys, each with a single dinosaur. Inflatable dinosaurs may be obtained from a science museum gift shop or other children's specialty stores. Make the boulders from 18" x 18" blocks of foam purchased from an upholstery shop or fabric store. Carve them into rocky shapes with an electric knife, and then color them with brown spray paint.

Dino Mural

Cut open and flatten a refrigerator box. Sketch a giant prehistoric mural in pencil, and then fill it in with paint. Include a volcano with red hot lava (red glitter) flowing down the sides, exotic plant life, a soaring pterodactyl, and one large dinosaur with a hole where its face would be. Families can take turns having their pictures taken. One person stands behind the mural with her face poking through the hole while other family members pose around the dinosaur.

Guess My Name

Make two photocopies of a dinosaur from a coloring book. Glue one picture, without the dinosaur name, on the front of a large piece of folded tagboard. Glue the second copy on the inside, along with the name and any other descriptive information. Mount the tagboard on the wall at children's eye level. Parents and children try to guess the dinosaur's name. They can see if they are correct by opening up the folded tagboard. Make extra sheets for the children to color. Construct at least five tagboards using the children's favorite dinosaurs.

Games
Set up tables with some of the many commercially produced dinosaur activities, such as sewing cards, flannel figures, matching dinosaurs, and giant floor puzzles.

Paleontologist Playground
Arrange large-muscle equipment (slide, rocking boat, climber, balance beam) in one corner to make a paleontologist playground.

Building with Boulders
Fill brown grocery bags with crumpled newspaper and tape them shut. The children can build caves with them.

ATTIRE

Snaggletooth tiger vests can be made from full-sized grocery bags (see illustration, page 27). It is important to start with the bag properly folded. Lay the bag flat and then fold the bottom in half so that both sides of the bag are fully exposed. Starting at the middle of one side, use a scissors to cut at an angle through the bottom and to a point that is approximately 2 inches from the opposite side. Next, open up the bag. On the uncut side, cut a child-sized, circular armhole about 2 inches from the bottom of the bag. The bottom now forms the shoulder of the vest. Fold the pointed section of the shoulder in toward the armhole. Make the bottom edge jagged. Let the children paint them in their own designs. Make the costumes ahead of time so they can be worn to the party.

DECORATIONS

Cut giant, palm-like leaves from large sheets of green construction paper and hang them from the ceiling. Label each activity with a large sign.

ENTERTAINMENT

Call the participants together for a large circle time. Play Parent's Choice Award winner *Dinosaur Rock*, an audiotape of singing dinosaurs with scientifically accurate information, by Michele Valeri and Michael Stein (available by calling 1-800-331-3761). To ensure full participation, familiarize the children with the music and songs a few weeks before the event. Have a parent circulate during the party dressed up in a dinosaur costume. Our program purchased the fabric and pattern which were used by a grandparent volunteer who sewed the costume.

REFRESHMENTS

Keep it simple. Serve juices and cookies. Label them "Prehistoric Punch" and "Cretaceous Cookies."

Veggie Soup Soirée (Swah-Ray)

Health experts recommend that we eat at least five servings of vegetables a day. What could be healthier and more friendly than sharing a big bowl of vegetable soup? The children donate a variety of fresh vegetables ahead of time. On the day of the event, staff and volunteers make the soup. Use the reproducible example to make invitations for this event (see page 75).

ACTIVITIES

Veggie Prints

Fill shallow pie tins with tempera paint. Dip vegetables into the paints and then press them onto white paper. For example, dip broccoli (cut lengthwise) into green paint, onions (cut in half) into white paint, unripened tomatoes (cut in half) into red paint, and carrots (cut lengthwise) into orange paint. Or let the children choose their own colors. You can also make the prints on 100 percent cotton dish towels or T-shirts, but you will need acrylic paints. When working with a T-shirt, slip a piece of cardboard inside so the paint won't bleed through to the back. It takes about 30 minutes to dry. Wait 24 hours before washing the items in cold water with a mild detergent. Be sensitive to the views of those who consider it inappropriate to use food for anything but eating. Discuss their concerns with them, and decide whether to do this activity. I feel that it is acceptable, in our society, to use food in children's activities, because it is plentiful, inexpensive, nontoxic, and often reusable.

Veggie Place Mats

Have the children cut out pictures of their favorite vegetables from old magazines and seed catalogs. They can glue them on construction paper, and the parents can cover them with clear contact paper.

Play "Fruit or Vegetable?"

Put a collection of plastic fruits and vegetables in a basket. Label one grocery bag "fruits" and the other "vegetables." Attach pictures of vegetables and fruits to the grocery bags to illustrate the labels. The children can sort the plastic fruits and vegetables into the appropriate bags.

Dramatic Play

Set up a play area to look like the produce department in a grocery store.

REFRESHMENTS

You will need some volunteers to prepare the fresh vegetables and put them into a pot of vegetable or chicken stock to make the soup. Also serve cheese and crackers or grilled cheese sandwiches.

BOOKS

Growing Vegetable Soup, by Lois Ehlert (San Diego: Harcourt, 1987).
Stone Soup, by Marcia Brown (New York: Atheneum, 1947).
The Vegetables Go to Bed, by Christopher King (New York: Crown, 1994).

Sweet Dreams Jammy Party

Bedtime can often be trying for parents and children. This special event turns a chore into a nightly magical journey. The book *Sweet Dreams for Little Ones: Bedtime Fantasies to Build Self-Esteem* by Michael Pappas (Nashville: Winston, 1982) is a must-read. This book shows the power of visualization (using our imaginations to control ourselves) to reach goals and to learn new skills. Make invitations for this event from the reproducible example (see page 75).

ATTIRE

Pajamas *(children only!).*

ACTIVITIES

Star Wands
Children use markers, ribbons, and glitter to decorate two star shapes precut from construction paper. An adult inserts the end of a plastic straw between the stars and staples them together.

Blanket Pictures
Each child draws a self-portrait on a piece of 9" x 12" construction paper. An adult then places a square of fabric (approximately 5" x 5") over the picture, so that the head is showing, and glues one edge of the square to the paper. The fabric now looks like a blanket that can be lifted to cover and uncover the drawing of the child.

Story Corner
Provide a cozy story corner stocked with favorite bedtime stories like *Goodnight Moon, Grandfather Twilight,* and *There's a Nightmare in My Closet.* The parents can read to the children.

Kiddy Quilts
Let the children design their own quilts by gluing precut fabric squares on a sheet of 9" x 12" construction paper.

ENTERTAINMENT

Everyone lays down with their eyes closed while a volunteer dressed as a fairy godmother or godfather reads a story from *Sweet Dreams for Little Ones.* These stories are visualization exercises in which the listener is guided through imagery that creates warmth and happiness before sleep. The volunteer fairy godmother or godfather should also talk about scary dreams and ask the children to think of actions they can take if they have a bad dream or feel afraid at bedtime. Then read the book *Go Away, Big Green Monster.* Tell the children to use their star wands to chase bad dreams away. Also encourage them to talk to their parents about scary dreams, since the dreams may provide clues to the children's fears. If children are unwilling to discuss their dreams or say "I can't remember," parents should ask them to draw a picture. The artwork may speak volumes. The volunteer godmother or godfather can end the visit with a touch of the wand, a sprinkling of fairy dust (glitter), and a positive affirmation for each child.

MUSIC	*Globalullabies*, by Freyda Epstein.
	Baby Songs Good Night, by Hap Palmer.
	Celtic Lullaby, by Margie Butler.
	Barney's Sleepytime Songs, by EMI Records.

BOOKS	*Goodnight Moon*, by Margaret Wise Brown (New York: Harper, 1947).
	Sweet Dreams for Little Ones: Bedtime Fantasies to Build Self-Esteem, by Michael Pappas (Nashville: Winston, 1982).
	Grandfather Twilight, by Barbara Berger (New York: Philomel, 1984).
	There's a Nightmare In My Closet, by Maurice Sendak (New York: Dial, 1985).
	Dreamland, by Mary Chapin Carpenter (New York: Harper, 1996).
	Time for Bed, by Mem Fox (San Diego: Harcourt, 1993).
	Sleep Baby Sleep, by Michael Hague (New York: Morrow, 1994).
	Dreamcatcher, by Audrey Osofsky (New York: Orchard, 1992).
	Go Away, Big Green Monster, by Ed Emberley (Boston: Little Brown, 1992).
	The Underbed, by Cathryn Clinton (Intercourse, PA: Good Books, 1990).
	Sleep Tight, by B.G. Hennesy (New York: Viking, 1992).

DECORATIONS	Cut large and small stars from cardboard or tagboard and cover with aluminum foil. Also make a smiling moon and hang from the ceiling with white twinkle lights.

REFRESHMENTS	Serve star-shaped cookies and milk.

WINTER EVENTS

Gifts from the Heart

This is a great event to hold around the holidays. Families make gifts to give to their loved ones. The event puts the focus on giving instead of on spending and getting. Provide a grocery bag to each family for carrying home their treasures. Set up tables with plenty of supplies for each kind of gift. Each person can decide on which gifts they would like to make. Begin collecting such necessary items as mayonnaise jars, buttons, costume jewelry, and whatever else you need as soon as possible. Ask the parents to check with friends and relatives. You'll be surprised at the great response you will get. In planning your gift activities, try to be culturally sensitive to the population you serve. Make sure there is something for everyone. Invitations to the event can be made from the reproducible example (see page 75).

GIFT ACTIVITIES

Fantastic Frames
Buy inexpensive, precut picture frames from S&S Arts and Crafts catalog (1-800-243-9232), or cut out your own frames from tagboard paper. Decorate with popcorn or old buttons. Use white glue.

Switch Covers
Purchase very inexpensive plates for electric wall switches (about fourteen cents each). Decorate with puffy paints or Elmer's Glitter Glue.

Little Angel Ornaments
Using the pattern on page 81, cut wings out of tagboard ahead of time. Have the children decorate them with glue sticks and glitter. Later, the parents can cut out a photograph of their child's face and glue it between the wings, adding a metallic string or ribbon for hanging.

Tzedakah *(tsah-DAH-kah)*
Giving to others is one of the joys of Hanukkah. The Hebrew word *tzedakah* means "justice" and a tzedakah box is used to collect coins that will be donated to charity. Supply coffee cans or milk cartons (with a slit in each top) to be decorated with wallpaper scraps, glue, and markers.

Stationery
Provide four envelopes and four pieces of plain paper to each child. The children can decorate them with rubber stamps. Bundle the papers and envelopes together with some pretty ribbon.

Heart Ornaments or Necklaces
Prepare hearts shaped from baker's clay ahead of time. (See recipe on next page.) The children can paint them and sprinkle them with glitter. Add enough ribbon to make either an ornament or a necklace.

Recipe for Baker's Clay:

4 cups unsifted, all-purpose flour
1 cup salt
1 1/2 cups cold water

Mix, knead, and roll out the dough, which should not be sticky. Cut shapes with cookie cutters. Use a straw to create a hole at the top of the heart. Bake shapes for 50 to 60 minutes at 300 degrees.

Treasure Jars

Use white glue to fasten bits and pieces of donated costume jewelry to the lids of short, wide-mouthed glass jars. The jars can be used to store jewelry and other collectibles.

Designer Glassware

Turn glass mayonnaise jars into keepsake vases. Or, if available, use inexpensive clear glass cups or glass plates. Have the children paint the glass with PermEnamel, a product by Delta, available at most craft stores. Paint only on the backs of plates and only on the outside of cups and jars. The paint air-dries, is super tough, dishwasher-safe, and non-toxic. You can use it on tile, glass, pottery, mirrors, and ceramics.

Wrapping Paper

Dip star-shaped sponges into shallow pie tins filled with silver and gold tempera paints. Print onto blue tissue paper for some heavenly gift wrap.

Place a sponge in a pie tin and soak it with yellow or orange tempera paints. Then roll ears of corn across the sponge and then onto sheets of green tissue paper to make Kwanzaa wrapping paper.

Paint sprigs of evergreen branches (such as pine or spruce) with green tempera paint and arrange them on a sheet of colored tissue paper or plain brown wrapping paper. Lay newspaper on top of the arrangement and press firmly to get a naturally beautiful print on the tissue paper. You can reuse the sprigs, but use a clean sheet of newsprint each time.

DECORATIONS   A large evergreen tree (fire codes usually dictate an artificial one) is decorated with mittens and other useful items that have been donated that evening or collected beforehand. After the event, the mittens can be given to a charitable organization. Children can place canned goods for local foodshelves under the tree. These items can also be collected during the month prior to the event.

REFRESHMENTS   Provide cookies, hot chocolate with whipped cream, or heated fruit juice, such as apple cider mixed with cranberry juice and garnished with orange slices.

BOOKS   *Ask Mr. Bear*, by Marjorie Flack (New York: Collier, 1932).

Rainbow Fish, by Marcus Pfister (New York: North-South, 1992).

Giving, by Shirley Hughs (Cambridge, MA: Candlewick, 1993).

Winter Getaway

For those of us living in parts of the country where we experience real winter, a break from the weather can be a necessary thing. Since many people cannot afford to fly to the Caribbean, this special event will be greatly appreciated! Invitations can be prepared from the reproducible example (see page 75).

ACTIVITIES

Door Prize
Solicit a trip from the airlines; you may get lucky. You are more likely, however, to succeed in getting a local hotel to donate an overnight stay.

Dramatic Play
Set up an area with used airline tickets, old suitcases, clothes, straw hats, and child-sized sunglasses.

Sand Table
Fill the sand table with shells, beach shovels, and buckets. Sprinkle blue glitter into the sand. The children can hunt for shells.

Pineapple
Stuff brown paper lunch bags 2/3 full with newspaper. Use a bread twister to tie the top. Paint yellow triangles and brown crisscrosses on the sides. Paint the top green. When it is dry, cut the top to look like pineapple leaves.

Musical Islands
Make islands shaped out of cardboard, newspaper, or mats. Play island music. When the music stops, everyone retreats to the island of his or her choice.

ATTIRE
Wear warm weather clothes underneath normal winter clothes (which can be removed at the event). Ask parents to bring a beach towel to sit on.

DECORATIONS
Get posters of tropical destinations from a travel agency or commercial airline. Make giant pineapples out of large grocery bags (see instructions above) and hang them from the ceiling.

ENTERTAINMENT
Try to hire musicians who specialize in tropical music. Or check out fun tropical music from the library. Dance to the "Limbo Rock," a song from *Party Dance Favorites* (The Special Music Company, 1989). This is a great CD that includes other favorites like "The Bunny Hop," "The Hokey Pokey," "The Chicken Dance," and many more!

REFRESHMENTS
Serve pineapple juice and macaroons.

Meet the Artist

Parents will thoroughly enjoy viewing the pure creativity of their children's art when it is put on display at a real art opening. This event builds self-esteem and allows each child to shine. Each child should choose their favorite piece of artwork for the show. Display the piece along with the reproducible form on page 82, which has a space for a photograph of the "artist." The show is much more impressive if the artwork is displayed professionally, rather than just taped to a wall. A couple weeks ahead of time, gather up refrigerator boxes and paint them solid colors to complement the decor of the room. Mount each piece of art on construction paper and staple them onto the side of one of the refrigerator boxes. Each box can display a lot of art. Afterwards, fold up the boxes and store for use at another time.

At the event, offer some tips to the parents on ways to curate their child's artwork. For example, suggest that they ask their child to make a collage out of several pieces of his work. Or the parents might photo-reduce several pieces onto one page, date it, and file. They also might take pictures of their kitchen refrigerator, or the place where they display their art, and archive the photo. Or they can shrink art on a copy machine to make stationery, jewelry, or badges. Use the reproducible example to make invitations for this event (see page 75).

ACTIVITIES

Art Badges
Supply white paper and pencils for the children to draw on. Use a badge-maker to make original buttons with reduced photocopies of the drawings. Check crafts and hobby stores, or call for a Badge-A-Minit Starter Kit (1-800-223-4103).

Dramatic Play
Set aside an area for an art studio with plenty of watercolor paints, paper, materials for collages, and playdough.

Decorations
Put up a sign that says "ART GALLERY." Tie several helium balloons together on a string that is longer than the height of the boxes. Attach the string to a weight and place it on the floor of the box, in the middle, so that the balloons will be streaming out of the open top of the box.

ENTERTAINMENT

Play classical music in the background.

REFRESHMENTS

Provide edible paint for the children to decorate large plain sugar cookies. Make the edible paint by blending 2 cups of sifted confectioners' sugar with 1/4 cup milk and 1/4 cup light corn syrup. Store in airtight containers. Just prior to using, divide the paint into paper cups and tint with food coloring. Thoroughly clean all paint off the brushes, and then run them through a dishwasher so they are sanitized before the children use them to frost the cookies.

Winter Frolic

Children are naive when it comes to winter—they actually love it! Not that I don't. It's just that after a lifetime in Minnesota, I no longer relish, as they do, rolling around in the snow, making snowmen and snow angels, and catching snowflakes. They believe that the crystalline patterns on the windows are painted by a little elf named Jack Frost. So celebrate along with them! Make invitations for this event from the reproducible example (see page 75).

ACTIVITIES

Stuffed Mittens
Precut large mitten shapes from sheets of newspapers. Parents can staple four shapes together, two on each side for strength, leaving an opening for stuffing the mitten with crumpled newspaper. Then staple the opening shut. Finally, the children paint the mitten with tempera paint. Have plenty of grocery bags on hand for carrying home the mitten in case the paint is not dry.

Toboggan Rides
Weather permitting, give rides across the snow. Avoid hills.

Snow People
Snow people are made by gluing large, medium, and small paper doilies onto a large piece of manila paper. Provide markers and glue sticks. Ribbon scraps can be used to create scarves, and aluminum foil and construction paper scraps make lovely hats, eyes, and so forth.

Playdough Snow
The children can make snow people and animals out of white playdough. Give them buttons, tree twigs, leaves, pipe cleaners, jewelry scraps, seeds, bottle caps, metal washers, and small rubber fish to help them come to life. You will be amazed at the intensity of the children's efforts and the detail contained in their creations.

Jack Frost Hats

Ahead of time, cut half-circles from 12" x 18" manila paper. The children decorate them with small paper doilies, chalk, glitter, and glue. When they are finished, an adult shapes the half-circle into a cone by joining the ends of the straight side, adjusting it to the size of the child's head, and taping it closed.

Real Snowballs

Fill the water table or large plastic tub with snow. The children should wear mittens when they play in it. No snow? Fill the tub with ice cubes for the children to use in building ice castles.

DECORATIONS   Have the children decorate large, white paper doilies to look like snowflakes. Use pastel chalks, glue sticks, and glitter. Also drape yards of sheer fabric from the ceiling and around the entire room.

VIDEOS   *The Snowman*, by Raymond Briggs (Weston Woods, 1993).

Snowplows at Work (Bill Aaron Productions, 1994). (1-800-575-7669)

The Snowstorm, by Richard Scarry (Polygram Video, 1993).

BOOKS   *The Mitten*, by Jan Brett (New York: Putnam, 1989).

The Night the Moon Blew Kisses, by Lynn Manuel (Boston: Houghton, 1996).

Snowballs, by Lois Ehlert (San Diego: Harcourt, 1995).

The Snowy Day, by Ezra Jack Keats (New York: Viking, 1962).

Babies Love Winter Days, by Harold Roth (New York: Grosset & Dunlap, 1986).

When Winter Comes, by Robert Mass (New York: Scholastic, 1993).

REFRESHMENTS   Serve hot chocolate and snowballs made from white cupcakes and white frosting sprinkled with coconut.

Dad and Me

Fathers need special time that is set aside just for them and their children. Children who do not have their fathers available can invite male friends or relatives. Invitations to the event can be made from the reproducible example (see page 75).

ACTIVITIES

House Painting
Wearing one of dad's old shirts, the child can paint walls covered with butcher paper using buckets of tempera paint, drop cloths, rollers, and wide house-painting brushes.

Face Shaving
Beforehand, use duct tape to fasten 9-inch balloons to a table. Secure them by placing a tagboard collar (about 2 inches high) around the bottom. Draw faces using permanent markers. At the event, dads and children can apply shaving cream to the face and shave it with old-fashioned shavers (blades removed). Provide paper towels and small bowls of water to rinse off the shavers.

Shoot Hoops
The toy manufacturing company Little Tykes makes a great freestanding basketball hoop called Little Tikes Easy Score Basketball that is adjustable for toddlers and preschoolers. It is available at many department stores, or you can call Nasco, a school supply store (1-800-558-9595). Provide extra balls so that more than one can shoot at the same time.

Painter's Hats
Painter's hats are very inexpensive at large home improvement stores. The children decorate them with markers, glitter glue, and puffy paints.

Dad-and-Me Handprints
Provide a blended mixture of liquid soap and tempera paint of any color. Dad and his children each paint one of their palms. They then press their hands on a piece of construction paper, making side-by-side handprints. Frame the print by gluing it onto a larger piece of construction paper.

Car Painting
Children dip small, plastic toy cars into pie tins partially filled with (black) tempera paint. Rolling the wheels across large sheets of butcher paper, the children enjoy making tire tracks and roads.

ATTIRE

The children wear dad's old workshirt.

VIDEOS

Just Me and My Dad, by Mercer Mayer (Library Video Company).
Workout With Daddy and Me (Family Home Entertainment, 1992).

BOOK

Daddy and Me, by Neil Ricklen (New York: Simon & Schuster, 1988).

REFRESHMENTS

Serve rootbeer floats.

Wild Rumpus

Parents will appreciate the opportunity for their children to completely cut loose in a safe environment. Invitations can be prepared from the reproducible example (see page 75).

ACTIVITIES

Free-For-All
Cut a refrigerator box lengthwise into two halves and secure the ends with duct tape. Fill each box with about 9 inches of crumpled-up newspaper. Allow two children at a time to dive, jump, and throw rolled up newspapers around inside each box.

Crazy Headgear
Provide precut tagboard headbands. Have the children decorate them with markers. Use duct tape to fasten two pipe cleaners to the front of the headband. Crumple a piece of aluminum foil around the top of each pipe cleaner.

Mystery Tunnel
Construct a long tunnel out of cardboard boxes taped together with duct tape. Give flashlights to the children to light their way as they crawl through.

Monkey Jump
Set out several mini-trampolines for the children to jump on. Borrow them from families or other programs. Be sure to closely supervise and spot-check the jumper.

Mega Bubbles
Fill a plastic wading pool with 2 inches of water. Add one cup of Dawn or Joy dishwashing soap. Use a commercially made giant bubble wand or try a hula hoop to make the bubbles. If this sounds too wild, you may prefer to purchase No-Spill Bubble Tumblers from Kids, Inc. (1-800-545-5437). They are made especially for young children so that they can blow their own bubbles with no mess.

Streamer Toss
The children roll up crepe paper streamers and throw them across a designated area.

ATTIRE Wear crazy clothes!

DECORATIONS Hang streamers everywhere and rent a bubble machine.

VIDEO *Where the Wild Things Are*, by Maurice Sendak (Weston Woods, 1976).

REFRESHMENTS Provide animal crackers and juice.

BOOK *Where the Wild Things Are*, by Maurice Sendak (New York: Harper, 1963).

Parent Makeovers

We have a poster in our parenting classroom that says "Children's needs are best met by parents whose needs are met." This event focuses on helping parents to look and feel their best! Use the reproducible example to make invitations for this event (see page 75).

Solicit large and small beauty salons and barber shops for donations of gift certificates or discounts on haircuts. Offer door prizes that include a haircut, makeup, and free advice from several makeover experts. Ask merchants who sell makeup or health and beauty products to set up booths. Invite color advisors, nutritionists, massage therapists, and exercise and other health consultants to be available for questions at the event.

Provide a "mental makeover" to hardworking parents by presenting a main speaker who has a positive and upbeat message. If you have access to a person with computer knowledge, you might be able to offer free computerized analyses related to health and beauty.

Provide child care. If you do not have the resources to provide for all children, then restrict the child care to preschoolers, since parents can place infants and toddlers in strollers and take them along. Let parents know that they must sign up in advance and that there is a limit to the number of children you can serve.

REFRESHMENTS   Provide bran muffins and serve fresh carrot and fruit juices prepared in an electric juice machine.

Gym Night/A.M. Aerobics

Exercise is one of the least expensive, most effective ways to maintain our health, so any event that encourages physical activity will be of great benefit. Both of these events could be held yearly or weekly. They are most popular when the weather is either too hot or too cold to be outside. Maintain a welcoming, informal atmosphere so that new families will feel comfortable stopping by to visit. Once you get organized, both events are simple and fun to do. Make invitations for these events from the reproducible example (see page 75).

A.M. AEROBICS

Hold this event early in the day or on a Saturday morning. A loud and energetic person should lead the class. A local college may be able to supply an intern who is pursuing a degree in physical education. Or you might play an exercise videotape. Decide on a class format by talking to the parents and incorporating their preferences. The whole class period can be spent with the parent and child together, starting with large group exercise followed by free play. Or parents and children can start out together, and then the adults continue to exercise while the free play is supervised by staff.

GYM NIGHT

This event will draw more family members since it is held in the evening. Fill an ample area with as much large-muscle equipment as possible and let everyone come and play as they please. If your supply of large-muscle equipment is limited, here are some ideas to expand the available activities:

- Create tunnels out of cardboard boxes. Make one long tunnel or several shorter ones using duct tape to connect them.
- Make bowling pins from clear plastic 16 oz. soda pop bottles. Fill with brightly colored beads, and tape shut.
- Pass out bright, sheer pieces of fabric for scarf dancing.
- Pass out feathers that the children can try to keep afloat by blowing on them.
- Play "Stepping Stones" with building blocks. Children try to maintain their balance while they step from one block to another.
- Create a balance beam or tightrope by laying down a line of colored tape on the floor. Make it a little more challenging by asking the children to carry a parasol as they walk across the "rope."
- Throw balls or beanbags into decorated laundry baskets or cardboard boxes.

DECORATIONS

Use the covers of health and fitness magazines to make posters.

MUSIC	*Bear-Robics*, by The Teddy Bear Band (Richard Alan Productions, 1992). (612-861-3570, http://www1.minn.net/~bearband)
	Mousersize (Walt Disney Productions, 1992).
VIDEO	*Teeny Time Tune-Ups* (Anthony Paul Inc.). (Available from Redleaf Press, 1-800-423-8309.)
REFRESHMENTS	Serve fruit juice and fat-free cookies. Also have plenty of water. Most people do not drink enough. Many people who feel fatigued are really dehydrated and just need more water!

Purple Crayon Party

Children who attend this party will never forget the color purple! You could also select some other color. If you decide to do more than one color, choose from the primary colors. Invitations to the event can be made from the reproducible example (see page 75).

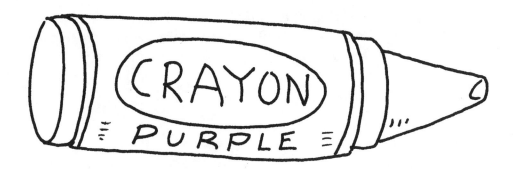

ACTIVITIES

Prospecting for Purple

The children pretend to be prospectors panning for purple pebbles! Ahead of time, lay large pebbles on sheets of newspaper, and brush or spray with purple paint. Dry the pebbles and then mix them into the sand table or sandbox. Provide plastic sieves and scoops so the children can prospect for the purple pebbles.

Tracing

Pass out large sheets of butcher paper so parents can trace their children's bodies and other large objects such as chairs, balls, and toys. Use large purple crayons, of course!

Crayon Costumes

To make purple vests, prepare grocery bags ahead of time. Cut a round hole for the head out of the bottom, and round armholes out of the sides near the bottom. Then cut up the center of the front along the whole length of the bag and into the hole in the bottom. The children must paint these vests purple ahead of time and wear them to the event. Also, cut half-circle shapes from 12" x 18" purple construction paper. At the event, children decorate the half-circles with purple crayons. An adult then makes a cone-shaped hat by joining the ends of the straight side, adjusting to the size of the child's head, and taping the ends together.

Making Purple

Provide containers of blue- and red-colored water and empty containers for mixing.

Color Cube

Paint the inside of a large appliance box purple and cut an opening on one side for the children to crawl through. Fill with purple objects and mount pictures of purple things on the inside walls. Allow two children

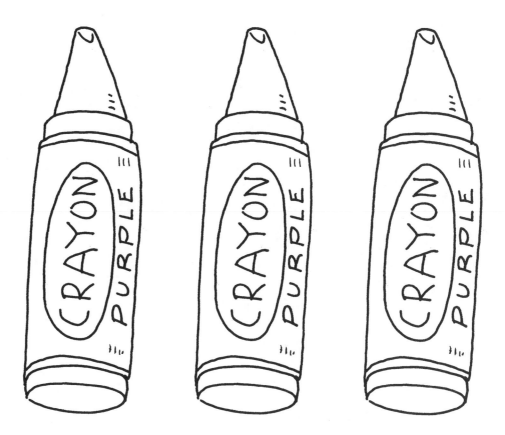

at a time inside and provide purple crayons and paper for them to color on. Set out a bowl of grape-flavored candies, but be certain it's not something children can choke on. The idea here is to give the children a place where they can explore and be immersed in a color that they can touch, see, taste, and smell.

ATTIRE	Ask that parents and children wear as much purple as possible.
DECORATIONS	Drape yards of purple sheer fabric across the ceiling.
VIDEO	*Harold and the Purple Crayon*, by Crockett Johnson (Weston Woods, 1969).
REFRESHMENTS	Provide a mixture of grape juice and apple juice (to cut down on staining) and vanilla wafers, which the children can top with purple frosting.
BOOK	*My Crayons Talk*, by Patricia Hubbard (New York: Scholastic, 1996).

SPRING EVENTS

Arbor Day Celebration

Back in the early 1880s, Nebraska was a treeless plain. When Julius Sterling Morton moved there from Detroit, he missed the beauty of trees. He also recognized that trees were needed for windbreaks, fuel, and building materials. This led him to establish Arbor Day, a holiday set aside for tree planting. National Arbor Day is designated as the last Friday in April. The date Arbor Day is celebrated in each of the fifty states varies (see page 49). It has been said that planting trees is an act of kindness that leaves a gift for future generations. Arbor Day celebrations give children an opportunity to help make the world a better place and learn about nature. Invitations can be prepared from the reproducible example (see page 75).

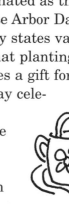

ACTIVITIES

Planting Trees
Contact the Department of Natural Resources, Department of Agriculture, or Forestry Association in your state. Everyone is welcome to information and, if you are a nonprofit organization, they may be able to supply you with seedlings to plant. For other sources of seedlings, contact garden centers and nurseries. For a free packet of information about Arbor Day, contact The National Arbor Day Foundation, 100 Arbor Avenue, Nebraska City, Nebraska 68410 (402-474-5655).

Leaf Matching
Press pairs of similar leaves in a telephone book for a couple of days. Then mount each leaf on a square of tagboard and cover it with clear contact paper. The children can try to match the pairs and identify them.

Spatter Pictures
Lay down newspaper and place a sheet of 12" x 18" manila paper on top of it. Have children arrange a variety of flattened leaves on the paper. Lay an old window screen over the arrangement, but don't let the screen

touch the leaves. Have children dip an old toothbrush into some thin tempera paint and rub it across the screen. The covered areas of the paper will remain unpainted, leaving the shapes of the leaves. Remove the screen and leaves, allowing the picture to remain flat while drying. Set up several screens, so the children will not have to wait long for their turns.

Body Trees
Lay children down on a large piece of butcher paper with their arms out, elbows bent straight up, fingers open, and legs together with feet turned out. Make sure to leave enough space above the head to add a collage of leaves. Use a crayon to trace the whole body except for the head. Then extend the tracing of the neck so that the body looks like a tree trunk and the arms like large branches. A sponge and paint can be used to create leaves, or glue on a collection of real leaves.

Identify Trees
Find or take photographs of trees in your neighborhood. Display them for parents and children to identify.

Earth Saver Project
Choose an outside area that needs cleaning up. Work on your own play area, a nearby empty lot, or a park. On the day of the event, pitch together to collect litter and plant trees and flowers.

Feely Bag
Fill a pillowcase with things from trees, such as pines cones, bark, leaves, nuts, and twigs. Children take turns trying to identify each item by only using their sense of touch.

ENTERTAINMENT Contact your local office of forestry, state forester, or the local office of the Department of Agriculture and ask about their Smokey the Bear or Woodsy Owl costumes. We found the Smokey costume to be spectacular, but very warm to wear.

VIDEO *Johnny Appleseed* (Rabbit Ears Productions, 1994).

REFRESHMENTS Serve commercially prepared maple leaf cookies and milk.

BOOKS *The Giving Tree*, by Shel Silverstein (New York: Harper, 1964).

Red Leaf, Yellow Leaf, by Lois Ehlert (San Diego: Harcourt, 1991).

A Tree Can Be, by Judy Nayer (New York: Scholastic, 1994).

ARBOR DAYS ACROSS THE NATION

State	Arbor Day	State Tree
Alabama	Last full week in February	Southern Pine
Alaska	Third Monday in May	Sitka Spruce
Arizona	Last Friday in April	Paloverde
Arkansas	Third Monday in March	Pine
California	March 7-14	California Redwood
Colorado	Third Friday in April	Blue Spruce
Connecticut	April 30	White Oak
Delaware	Last Friday in April	American Holly
District of Columbia	Last Friday in April	Scarlet Oak
Florida	Third Friday in January	Cabbage Palmetto
Georgia	Third Friday in February	Live Oak
Hawaii	First Friday in November	Kukui
Idaho	Last Friday in April	Western White Pine
Illinois	Last Friday in April	White Oak
Indiana	Last Friday in April	Yellow Poplar
Iowa	Last Friday in April	Oak
Kansas	Last Friday in March	Cottonwood
Kentucky	First Friday in April	Kentucky Coffeetree
Louisiana	Third Friday in January	Bald Cypress
Maine	Third full week in May	Eastern White Pine
Maryland	First Wednesday in April	White Oak
Massachusetts	April 28 - May 5	American Elm
Michigan	Last week in April	Eastern White Pine
Minnesota	Last Friday in April	Red Pine
Mississippi	Second Friday in February	Southern Magnolia
Missouri	First Friday in April	Flowering Dogwood
Montana	Last Friday in April	Ponderosa Pine
Nebraska	Last Friday in April	Cottonwood
Nevada, Southern	February 28	Singleleaf Pinyon
Nevada, Northern	April 23	Singleleaf Pinyon
New Hampshire	Last Friday in April	Paper Birch
New Jersey	Last Friday in April	Northern Red Oak
New Mexico	Second Friday in March	Pinyon
New York	Last Friday in April	Sugar Maple
North Carolina	First Friday following March 15	Pine
North Dakota	First Friday in May	American Elm
Ohio	Last Friday in April	Ohio Buckeye
Oklahoma	Last full week in March	Eastern Redbud
Oregon	First full week in April	Douglas Fir
Pennsylvania	Last Friday in April	Eastern Hemlock
Rhode Island	Last Friday in April	Red Maple
South Carolina	First Friday in December	Cabbage Palmetto
South Dakota	Last Friday in April	White Spruce
Tennessee	First Friday in March	Yellow Poplar
Texas	Last Friday in April	Pecan
Utah	Last Friday in April	Blue Spruce
Vermont	First Friday in May	Sugar Maple
Virginia	Second Friday in April	Flowering Dogwood
Washington	Second Wednesday in April	Western Hemlock
West Virginia	Second Friday in April	Sugar Maple
Wisconsin	Last Friday in April	Sugar Maple
Wyoming	Last Monday in April	Cottonwood
National Arbor Day	**Last Friday in April**	

Victorian Tea Party

Children are delighted by attending a tea party. Possible themes include royalty, springtime, dolls, full moon, or Valentine's, but I thought it would be different to put on a Victorian Tea Party. Use the reproducible example to make invitations for this event (see page 75).

ACTIVITIES

Top Hats

Make Victorian top hats by opening a grocery bag and folding back the open end to form a cuff about 3 inches high. Make a headband by stapling the ends of a 1-inch wide piece of elastic. Then tuck the circle of elastic inside the cuff. For a serious top hat appearance, paint it black, or for a more cheerful look, decorate it with tissue paper, buttons, old ribbons, or silk flowers.

FOLD BACK OPENING TO FORM CUFF

STAPLE 1" WIDE STRIP OF ELASTIC INSIDE CUFF

Victorian Fans

Give the children 9-inch paper plates that have been cut in half to look like fans. Provide the children with paper doilies, feathers, glue, scissors, and markers to decorate their fans.

"Real People" Paper Dolls

Make one photocopy each of pages 83 and 84. Cut out the copies to make one pattern for each doll shape. Then trace the shapes onto tagboard paper and cut them out, making enough for all of the children. You will need a clear photograph of a front view of each child's face. Make extra photocopies, because you will find them useful for a variety of other activities. Use a copy machine to enlarge or reduce the size of the photo to fit the cut-out doll. Cut out the face and glue it onto the doll's head. The children can dress the doll by coloring it and gluing on fabric scraps, buttons, lace, and ribbons. This activity requires a little work ahead of time, but you will enjoy the way it draws out the personality and culture of each child.

Necklaces

Make necklaces by stringing heart-shaped pasta on ribbon or by stringing doughnut-shaped colored breakfast cereal on licorice laces.

Soft Touch

This game, a version of "Duck, Duck, Gray Duck," was reportedly so popular with the Royal Court in England that no one got any work done, so the king banned it. In the preschool version, children sit in a circle. One player tiptoes around the circle and softly touches one of the others on the back. That person chases the toucher around the circle. The toucher then sits in the empty spot and the chaser becomes the new toucher.

Dress Up
Provide piles of dress-up clothes, old jewelry, purses, boas, and gloves in front of a childproof, full-length mirror.

Dollhouses
Set up several old-fashioned dollhouses.

ATTIRE	Encourage everybody to dress up and wear hats and gloves.
DECORATIONS	Use old lace curtains as tablecloths and decorate with large tissue flowers. Display a real tea set.
ENTERTAINMENT	Provide some lovely classical background music. At our Spring Tea Party, one of our moms played her flute.
REFRESHMENTS	Serve apple juice from a fancy teapot. Make finger sandwiches shaped by cookie cutters and top them with cream cheese and cucumbers, or with cream cheese and fruit jam. Provide disposable cups with handles so that they seem more like a real teacup.
BOOKS	*Miss Spider's Tea Party,* by David Kirk (New York: Scholastic, 1994).
	Victorian Fashion Paper Dolls from Harper's Bazaar, 1867-1898, by Theodore Menten (Mineola, NY: Dover, 1979).
	(You can cut out the dolls and outfits and then laminate or cover them with clear contact paper.)
	Victorian Houses Coloring Book, by Daniel Lewis (Mineola, NY: Dover, 1950).

Baby Shower

Throwing a baby shower for infants and toddlers in your community is a great way to welcome new families and familiarize them with your program. Contact local diaper services, baby stores, and department stores to solicit donations. Make invitations for this event from the reproducible example (see page 75).

ACTIVITIES
FOR BABIES
AND PARENTS

Handprints
Provide brushes and tempera paint mixed with liquid soap in equal parts. The parent paints the baby's hands and presses them onto a copy of the poem on page 85. When dry, mount the print on construction paper.

Infant Playground
Set up an area with washable mats, a safety mirror, and washable baby toys. Hang large pieces of colorful, soft, sheer fabric along a clothesline strung across the room. The infants and toddlers love the feel of crawling back and forth through the fabric.

Mini-Marathon
Infants and toddlers are separated from their parents by about a 10-foot distance. Parents try to coax their child to come to them.

Parenting Tips
Create an information sheet or a small booklet containing the latest parenting tips for parents to take home. Be sure to put your program's name, address, and telephone number on it!

Bubbles
Infants and toddlers love bubbles, so set up an area where parents and their children can blow bubbles.

ACTIVITIES
FOR OLDER
SIBLINGS

Dolly Stroll
Provide several toy baby carriages and set up a walking course for preschool-aged brothers and sisters to take dolls for a ride.

Bathing Babies
Fill a water table with warm soapy water, sponges, and washable baby dolls.

Clothesline
String a low clothesline across the room. Place plenty of baby things (bibs, sleepers, and booties) and clothespins in a basket, so the siblings can hang them up.

Decorations
Hang umbrellas and pink, blue, and mint green streamers from the ceiling. Display giant tissue flowers and storks. Also set up toy (or real) watering cans filled with artificial flowers, or tape helium balloons to the inside bottoms of the cans.

ENTERTAINMENT   Play lullaby music.

REFRESHMENTS   Serve commercially prepared sheets of birthday cake and punch.

BOOKS   *Welcome, Little Baby*, by Aliki Brandenberg (New York: Greenwillow, 1987).

More, More, More, Said The Baby, by Vera B. Williams (New York: Greenwillow, 1990).

Peter's Chair, by Ezra Jack Keats (New York: Harper, 1967).

On the Day I Was Born, by Debbi Chocolate (New York: Scholastic, 1995).

On the Day You Were Born, by Debra Frasier (San Diego: Harcourt, 1991).

Alice in Wonderland

The classic imaginative tale of *Alice in Wonderland* endears children as well as adults. We combined this theme with a Spring Tea Party one year, and everyone had a "very curious time." Invitations to the event can be made from the reproducible example (see page 75).

ACTIVITIES

Croquet for Kids

Provide tennis balls and toy brooms with large ribbons tied around them for mallets. Cut large U-shaped holes from one side of cardboard boxes and paint them bright colors. Turn the boxes upside-down and line them up against a wall. Use dividers to create alleys to prevent interference while several children play at the same time. The children use the broom to stroke the ball into the box.

Painting the Roses Red

Collect as many plastic roses as you can (from garage sales, the Goodwill, or parents) and lay them on sheets of newspaper. The children paint them shades of red with tempera paint mixed with liquid soap. When they all have been painted, rinse them off and start over again.

White Rabbit Chase

An energetic volunteer dresses as a white rabbit. Create the costume from a dresscoat (with tails, if available), a large pocket watch, white gloves, white shirt and pants, and a bow tie. Wear white makeup and rabbit ears, or wear a white rabbit mask. Set up a safe area where three or four children at a time can try to catch the rabbit.

Matching Cards

Using two identical decks of playing cards, create pairs of matching face cards (value and suit). Place the cards on several serving trays so that children can try to match them up.

What's Inside?

Fill old, clean socks with a variety of objects, such as an old watch, a stuffed white rabbit, a plastic rose, and white gloves. Children reach inside and guess what the object is by feeling it.

Queen of Hearts Tarts

Tarts are cookie-like pastry shells filled with raw or cooked fruit, often accompanied by a custard or cream filling. Set out playdough, rolling pins, and tart tins (available in some housewares departments) so the children can make tarts for the Queen.

Matching Teacups

Set up a small table for a simple tea. Provide several different kinds of inexpensive teacups with matching saucers. Mix up the cups and saucers and let the children try to match them.

Petting Zoo
Invite a real white rabbit, baby pig (from a farm), and a very friendly smiling cat to the party.

DECORATIONS   From a large cardboard box, cut a door just big enough for a child to crawl through. Place it at the entrance to the event and direct the children to creep through it on their way to "Wonderland." Hang Chinese lanterns around the room; they are very colorful and inexpensive. Purchase them at a party supply store and use them over and over. As a centerpiece for the tables, use oversized tissue flowers made ahead of time by the children.

ENTERTAINMENT   Have a volunteer dress as Alice. I put together a blond pageboy wig, a solid blue long-sleeved dress with a shirt gathered at the waist ($3.00 at the Goodwill), a white gathered apron, white tights, black shoes, and a black headband for her costume. Alice can circulate around the party and talk to the children. Include a circle time at which you sing the children's favorite songs.

REFRESHMENTS   Provide fruit-filled cookies and cider in paper teacups.

BOOK   *Alice in Wonderland*, by Walt Disney (New York: Golden, 1951).

Birthday Bash

At this birthday bash, everyone's birthday is celebrated at the same time. No one is left out, so those children whose birthdays occur when the program is out of session do not miss celebrating with their school chums. Invitations can be prepared from the reproducible example (see page 75).

see page 75

ACTIVITIES

Giant Fake Cakes
Make a giant cake by stacking three cardboard boxes of various sizes on top of each other. The largest box should be on the bottom, the medium one next, and the small one on the top. Tape them together with duct tape. Children frost the cake with pastel tempera paint thickened with soap flakes. They then add silk or plastic artificial flowers, or flowers made from tissue paper. To make birthday candles, roll 9" x 12" pieces of construction paper into cylinders, and tape. Add a tuft of red tissue paper and foil to the top to make it look like the candles are burning.

Guess What's Inside?
Wrap birthday gift boxes so the lids can come off. The children try to guess what is inside the boxes by shaking or otherwise examining them.

Make Balloon Bats
Pass out 9-inch paper plates to the children and let them decorate the plates with markers. When they are done, give each child a balloon and warn them about the dangers of choking. Direct the children to a large, sectioned-off area with plenty of space. The children can try to keep the balloon airborne by batting it with the "balloon bat."

Play "Little Limbo"
Place a broom across two chair backs. Play music. Line up the children and ask them to dance their way under the broom. Set up two or three brooms in succession so that once it gets going, anxious children will have a short wait.

Birthday Cake Frosting Fun
You will need shaving cream, food coloring, several large plastic bowls, empty plastic ketchup bottles, smooth plastic knives, and rubber spatulas. Fill several bowls with shaving cream and mix a different food coloring into each. Demonstrate to the children how to fill a ketchup bottle with shaving cream using a small spatula. Turn several empty bowls upside down (they are the birthday cakes) and let the children "frost" the cakes.

Nose Races
Put a dab of petroleum jelly on the tip of the children's noses. Have the children line up at a starting point. They must crawl, hop, or walk to a pile of cotton balls, where each of them tries to pick up a cotton ball with their noses and return to the starting line with it. Everyone laughs when the parents play.

DECORATIONS	Use balloons and streamers to decorate the room.
ENTERTAINMENT	Ask a volunteer to dress as a clown. Consider having the clown pass out stickers or treats to the children. Be aware that some infants and toddlers are frightened by clowns. Play "Happy Birthday." You may wish to purchase *Party Dance Favorites* by The Party Dance Band (The Special Music Company and Pair Records, 1989). There are many fun songs on this recording, including "Limbo" and "The Bunny Hop."
REFRESHMENTS	Serve birthday cake, milk, and coffee.
BOOKS	*On the Day You Were Born,* by Debra Frasier (San Diego: Harcourt, 1991).
	On the Day I Was Born, by Debbi Chocolate (New York: Scholastic, 1995).
	Happy Birth Day! by Robie H. Harris (Cambridge, MA: Candlewick, 1996).
	Happy Birthday, Moon, by Frank Asch (New York: Scholastic, 1982).
	Benny Bakes a Cake, by Eve Rice (New York: Greenwillow, 1981).

Garden Party

Gardening is a tremendous learning opportunity for children. They gain an appreciation for nature, learn responsibility, witness life cycles, and enjoy the fruits of their harvest, even if it is only a single tulip bulb or a handful of green beans. Use the reproducible example to make invitations for this event (see page 75).

ACTIVITIES

Gardening
Fill a water table or oblong plastic tub with sand, toy garden tools, artificial flowers, and flower pots. The children can plant and repot just like a real gardener.

The Seed Game
Buy packaged garden seeds. Empty the seeds out and mount the fronts of the packages on a piece of tagboard paper cut the same size as the package. Sprinkle the seeds on the tagboard side and cover the seed side and then the front of the package with clear contact paper. Lay the packages on a table, seed-sides up. The children guess each type of seed, turning over the packages to confirm their guesses. Choose seeds common to foods grown in your area.

Picket Fence Mural
Draw a white picket fence on butcher paper and tape it to a wall. The children draw or paint colorful flowers along the fence, making a garden mural.

Ask the Expert
Invite a knowledgeable representative from a local garden store to answer questions at an "Ask the Expert" booth.

Garden Stepping Stones
Children decorate their own stepping stones to be placed on a garden path or in their yard. Purchase a premixed bag of concrete. A 60-pound bag costs about $1.50. Follow the instructions on the bag. Pour the mixture into aluminum pie tins. The children can use a stick to write or draw things, or press leaves or shells to make a beautiful nature print. If they want to make a print of their hand or foot, lay a piece of plastic wrap across the concrete to avoid direct contact with the skin. When dry, pop the stepping stone out of the tin, and the child will have a lifetime keepsake.

Seeds
Give the children some carrot seeds, bean seeds, or a bulb that they can take home and plant. They will have extra fun growing Scarlet Runner Beans around a tepee trellis because the covered trellis becomes an unusual space for children to play in.

Plant Sale

Early spring is a great time for buying and selling plants. Work out an agreement with a wholesaler who distributes garden plants whereby your program will take orders for plants and you will share the profits. Take orders before the day of the event. The plants are then picked up at the event.

DECORATIONS   Hang giant tissue flowers made ahead of time by the children. Put several garden sprinkling cans on the food table and fill them with real plants.

REFRESHMENTS   Provide cupcakes with chocolate frosting sprinkled with crushed Oreo cookies to look like dirt. Add a gummy worm, crawling out of the "soil."

BOOKS   *Planting a Rainbow*, by Lois Ehlert (San Diego: Harcourt, 1988).

Alisons's Zinnia, by Anita Lobel (New York: Mulberry, 1990).

The Carrot Seed, by Ruth Krauss (New York: Scholastic, 1993).

NATURE HIKES

This event is held at a nature center, nearby park, farm, or wooded area. Use the reproducible example to make invitations for this event (see page 75). You create a theme and construct activities suited to the time of year. Often nature centers will plan hikes for families or groups. Here are some suggestions for hikes of your own.

Fall Outing

Collect and identify leaves, sort nuts, look for squirrels preparing for winter, identify migrating birds, and observe changes in the trees and foliage.

REFRESHMENTS   Serve crisp fall apples and candy corn.

BOOKS   *Fall*, by Ron Hirschi (New York: Dutton, 1991).

How Do You Know It's Fall? by Allan Fowler (Danbury, CT: Childrens Press, 1992).

Step Into Fall: A New Season, by Jane B. Moncure (Minneapolis: Child's World, 1990).

Winter Full Moon Walk

Observe a full moon and stars with telescopes made from paper towel, toilet tissue, or construction paper tubes. Children can decorate the tubes using markers and star stickers. Provide a real telescope to view the sky. Look for animal tracks in the snow.

REFRESHMENTS   Serve star cookies and hot chocolate.

BOOKS   *Mooncake*, by Frank Asch (New York: Scholastic, 1983).

Moondance, by Frank Asch (New York: Scholastic, 1993).

Regards to the Man in the Moon, by Ezra Jack Keats (New York: Aladdin, 1981).

Spring Birding

Make binoculars by removing the bottoms of two paper cups (not wax coated, if they are to be painted) and stapling them side-by-side so that the narrow parts of the cups are next to each other. Use a paper punch to put a hole on both sides of the narrow ends. String a length of yarn through the holes and out the top, and tie. The binoculars now can be worn around the neck. Go on a birding expedition. The children can observe and identify as many birds as possible. Maintain a list as you go along.

REFRESHMENTS   Provide cartons of juice and baggies containing a mixture of sunflower seeds and dried fruits.

BOOKS   *Are You My Mother?* by P. D. Eastman (New York: Random, 1960).

The Best Nest, by P. D. Eastman (New York: Random, 1968).

Over in the Meadow, illustrated by David A. Carter (New York: Scholastic, 1992).

Summer Evening Walk

Look for animals common to your area. Listen to crickets. Make a "bug bulb" by collecting as many fireflies as possible in a glass jar. Poke holes in the lid. Release them at the end of the night.

REFRESHMENTS   Provide cold lemonade and popcorn.

BOOKS   *The Very Lonely Firefly*, by Eric Carle (New York: Philomel, 1995).

The Very Quiet Cricket, by Eric Carle (New York: Philomel, 1990).

Fireflies, Fireflies Light My Way, by Jonathan London (New York: Viking, 1996).

Teddy Bear Picnic

Choose a favorite nearby park where people can meet. There are many ways to have a picnic. Either families can bring their own food, or the program might provide part of the meal (for example, sloppy joes or veggie burgers) and families bring something to share. Or just have a large potluck! Always provide the basics, like plates, napkins, cups, eating utensils, and something to drink, to make it easier on busy families. Make invitations for this event from the reproducible example (see page 75).

ACTIVITIES

Picnic Baskets

Cut off the top half of a brown grocery bag. Fold over the rim of the bottom half, forming a cuff of about 3 inches on the outside. Now make a handle by cutting a 6-inch wide strip along the circumference of the top part of the bag and folding it in half lengthwise. Then tuck the ends of the handle under the cuff on both sides and staple to the rim. The children decorate the baskets with crayons, markers, and pictures cut from seed and garden catalogs.

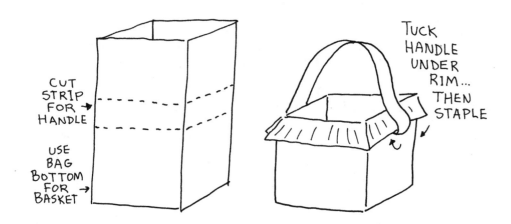

Teddy Ears

Use brown construction paper to make headbands with brown bear ears taped to them. The children color and try to write their names on them. When the children have completed their ears, put a black dot on their noses.

Toy Teddies

Invite the children to bring their own teddy bears or other favorite stuffed toys.

Play "Bear at the Picnic"

One child designated as the bear crawls around the playing area on his hands and knees. The other players walk around the bear in a clockwise rotation. When the bear is ready to surprise the players, he yells, "Bear at the Picnic!" and jumps up to try to tag another child, who then becomes the bear. The game is repeated.

Play "Bear in the Air"
The children grasp corners of blankets with toy teddy bears placed in the middle. They toss and bounce the bears.

ATTIRE   Playclothes are appropriate for these activities. Teddy bear headbands and black noses are created at the event.

ENTERTAINMENT   Hire live music. Make sure the music is familiar to the children. If you cannot afford to hire a musician, play favorite musical tapes.

MUSIC   *You're in the Show!* by The Teddy Bear Band (Richard Alan Productions, 1990). (1-888-822-2263, http://www1.minn.net/~bearband)

BOOK   *The Teddy Bears' Picnic*, by Jimmy Kennedy (New York: Holt, 1992).

Green Eggs and Ham Brunch

Green eggs may not appeal to expecting moms, but the children (like the book says) "do like green eggs and ham." Use imitation bacon bits instead of ham, mainly because they are easier to work with, but also in consideration of vegetarians who may be at the brunch. You might provide both versions. Invitations to the event can be made from the reproducible example (see page 75). Children can color the invitations green.

ACTIVITIES

Cat In the Hat Bow Ties
Precut giant bow tie shapes out of construction paper. Children decorate them with markers, scraps of fabric, ribbons, and glue. Attach the ties to the tops of the children's shirts with paper clips.

Make Green!
Have several trays, each holding three pitchers. Fill one pitcher half full with water dyed yellow from food coloring. Fill another half full with blue water. The third one is left empty and used by the children for mixing the blue and yellow water to make green. Monitor this activity, refilling the pitchers and mopping up as needed. Children enjoy pitching in to help clean, so have some sponges on hand for them to use.

Egg Hunt
The children hunt for plastic eggs. Hide them outside, inside the building, or in the sand table. Once the eggs are found, the children can sort them according to size or color, depending on the type of eggs.

Cat Hats
Open a grocery bag and fold back the open end to form a cuff about 3 inches high. Make a headband that fits the child's head by stapling the ends of a 1-inch wide piece of elastic. Then tuck the circle of elastic inside the cuff. The children paint horizontal stripes with tempera paint on all sides of the bag.

VIDEO

Green Eggs and Ham, by Dr. Seuss (New York: Random, 1994).

REFRESHMENTS

Serve green eggs and ham. Beat together eggs, milk, imitation bacon chips, and green food coloring. Pour into a large electric frying pan or wok to which a small amount of cooking oil has been added. Serve coffee, fruit juice, and commercially prepared baked goods that parents have brought.

BOOKS

Green Eggs and Ham, by Dr. Seuss (New York: Random, 1960).
Little Blue and Little Yellow, by Leo Lionni (New York: Astor-Honor, 1959).

Graduation Ceremony

My experience with this event is that the children have no idea what is going on, but they have fun, and the parents and other relatives who show up for this momentous ceremony love it. Make invitations for this event from the reproducible example (see page 75).

ACTIVITIES

Graduation Caps

Precut 2-inch wide strips of black construction paper about 20 inches long. Provide 9" x 9" squares of black construction paper, clear tape, scissors, stapler, and yarn. Parents make their child's cap at the event, before the ceremony begins. First form a construction paper headband, sized to fit on the top of the child's head. Then mount the headband onto one of the squares by taping inside the headband at several places. Tape a 12-inch piece of yarn to the center of the top to create the illusion of a tassel!

Yearbooks

These should be made ahead of time. Make enough copies of the four-face outline on page 86 so that each child may fill in one face outline to look like themselves with their name beneath it. The pages are passed to other children until each has filled in their likeness on one of the pages. I like to ask the children what they prefer most about school or what they would like to be when they grow up, and then write down the responses on their face pages. When the face pictures are completed, copy each one enough times to create a book for each child. Each book contains the faces of all the children. Take a group photograph and place copies of it with a list of all the children's names on the first page of each book. Present the yearbooks to the children at the graduation ceremony. They can then exchange autographs with their friends!

ATTIRE

Graduation caps made at the event.

DECORATIONS

Hang a huge banner that congratulates the class.

ENTERTAINMENT

The graduation ceremony is the highlight of the event. The master of ceremonies calls one child at a time up to the front of the room to shake hands and receive his or her diploma and yearbook. Make the diplomas from the reproducible form on page 87.

MUSIC

Check out *Pomp and Circumstance* from the library and play it at the ceremony.

REFRESHMENTS

Serve punch and cake.

SUMMER EVENTS

Fish Festival

Imagine sitting in the sun, relaxing and watching the world go by while waiting to catch the "Big One." Adults and children are intrigued by fishing. This event can also educate children about water safety and give those of us who don't fish a chance to see what all the fuss is about. Invitations can be prepared from the reproducible example (see page 75).

ACTIVITIES

Real Fish Prints

Make fish prints using a real fish that has been cleaned and scaled but otherwise left intact. Often, a local grocery store will supply one if you explain how it will be used and that it will not be eaten. Lay down plenty of newspaper to create a work space. Apply a thin layer of paint to the fish. Use tempera paint if printing onto tissue or other paper. Use acrylic paint to print onto 100 percent cotton fabric. Fabrics require at least 30 minutes to dry. After the event, washing with cold water will remove the fish smell.

Boat Safety

Ask around to find a canoe or boat owner who is willing to bring it in for the day of the event. The children sit in the canoe or boat and pretend to fish with toy poles and magnetic fish. Require children to wear life jackets while in the canoe or boat. Talk about boat safety.

Ask the Expert

Invite someone from the Department of Natural Resources, a sports and bait shop, or anyone who is knowledgeable about fish or fishing to attend the event and answer questions.

Identify Fish

Ask the Department of Natural Resources for a poster or pictures of fish from the lakes in your state. From two identical posters, cut out the fish to make a matching and identifying game. Whenever you make games like these, cover them with clear contact paper or have them laminated so they will hold up over time.

Play "Flying Fish"

Cut a large piece of blue flannel fabric into the shape of a pond. Cut fish shapes about 10 inches long out of lightweight paper. Lay the "fish" on the floor a few feet from the pond. Children use paper plates as fans to move the paper fish across the room and into the "pond."

Fishing Collage

Obtain past issues of fishing magazines from someone who has a subscription. Provide the children with glue sticks, markers, large sheets of manila paper, and scissors. Children cut out pictures and make a collage.

Fish Hats

LAYER THREE SHEETS OF LARGE GREEN TISSUE PAPER

LEAVE PIECE STICKING OUT FOR TAIL

ROLL UP LOOSE TISSUE PAPER AND STAPLE IN SEVERAL SECTIONS

These hats are really cute and easy to make. Layer three sheets of large green tissue paper on top of a child's head. The sheets will hang down alongside the child's head. Rotate each piece so that the corners are not lined up. Wrap several turns of masking tape around the child's head, trapping the sheets of tissue paper just above the eyebrows to form a snug headband. Leaving a piece sticking out from the back (this will be the fish tail), roll up the loose tissue paper and staple it in several sections, forming a tight rim around the rest of the head. The children glue wiggly eyes on both sides of the hat and add fins and scales by decorating with tissue paper scraps, glitter, and glue.

Digging for Worms

Fill the water table or a large plastic tub with soil and worms from a bait shop. Let the children dig for real worms.

ATTIRE
: Anything goes, but a flannel shirt and blue jeans are standard "fish fashion."

DECORATIONS
: Hang stuffed fish (made by the children ahead of time) from the ceiling. Cut large, simple fish shapes from four layers of newspaper for each fish. Staple around the shape and leave an opening to stuff with crumpled up newspaper. Stuff and staple the fish closed. The children paint them with tempera paint. Punch a hole at the top of the fish and add some string for hanging. Also drape inexpensive, sheer, blue fabric from the ceiling and around the fish.

REFRESHMENTS
: Serve goldfish crackers and juice. If you feel like cooking, get a deep fryer and serve "fish and chips."

BOOKS
: *Fishes,* by Brian Wildsmith (New York: Oxford UP, 1968).

  Swimmy, by Leo Lionni (New York: Scholastic, 1963).

  Rosie's Fishing Trip, by Amy Hest (Cambridge, MA: Candlewick, 1994).

  Loudmouth George and the Fishing Trip, by Nancy Carlson (Minneapolis: Carolrhoda, 1983).

Insect Extravaganza

Most children love hunting for insects and examining them. For those children who are afraid of bugs, this event can help alleviate some fear by associating the insects with fun activities. Use the reproducible example to make invitations for this event (see page 75).

ACTIVITIES

Caterpillars

Precut egg cartons in half to form caterpillar shapes. The children paint them with tempera paint and glue on wiggly eyes. An adult may add pipe cleaners for antennas.

Butterflies

Precut large butterfly shapes out of colorful tissue paper. The children decorate the wings with markers. An adult feeds the body of the butterfly into a spring-loaded clothespin and adds pipe cleaners for antennas. After all of the butterflies are made, the parents hide them so the children can go on a butterfly hunt and look for one they made.

Insect Pictures

Purchase a collection of rubber insect stamps. On a sheet of paper, the children draw grass, flowers, and ant hills and then use the rubber stamps to add insects to their pictures. Insect pictures also can be made by having the children collect real leaves, blades of grass, and twigs to glue onto their paper before adding the insects.

Bug Jugs

Under very close supervision, allow the children to use a hammer and nail to pound holes into the metal lids of empty glass jars. Provide a tough surface to pound on. The bug jugs can be used to collect insects during a bug hunting expedition. After the bug hunt, children display the insects they have caught and try to identify them. Release the insects before going home.

ENTERTAINMENT

Dance to Little Richard's version of "The Itsy Bitsy Spider" on Disney's *For Our Children* (Walt Disney, 1991). This tape has many wonderful songs that could be used at other events.

VIDEO

Bugs Don't Bug Us (Bo Peep Productions, 1991).

REFRESHMENTS

Serve "beetlejuice" (any juice) and gummy caterpillars.

BOOKS

The Grouchy Ladybug, by Eric Carle (New York: Harper, 1997).
The Very Hungry Caterpillar, by Eric Carle (New York: Philomel, 1981).
The Very Busy Spider, by Eric Carle (New York: Scholastic, 1984).
The Itsy Bitsy Spider, by Iza Trapani (New York: Scholastic, 1995).
I Love Spiders, by John Parker (New York: Scholastic, 1988).

Pet Show

Children love pets. In addition to being lots of fun, this event is also an opportunity for children to begin understanding the needs of animals. Make invitations for this event from the reproducible example (see page 75).

ACTIVITIES

Guest Speaker

Contact your local animal shelter or humane society to ask if they have an educational coordinator or volunteers who are willing to come to your event. They can talk to the families about caring for animals and maybe even bring a "visitor" or two.

Pet Parade

Children march in a parade with real animals, stuffed toys, or imagined pets.

Pet Responsibilities

In a large group, discuss the responsibilities of having a pet. Talk about what animals need and what we need to do to take proper care of them. Pets need food, water, space, shelter, and medical care. We need to treat them kindly, take time to care for them, and have money to pay for their food, licenses, shots, and other medical expenses.

Animal Exhibit

Hire a traveling petting zoo. Look for ones that are licensed and insured, have attractive pens that are safe and clean, have signs for each animal, and maintain proper vaccination schedules. We have hired several different petting zoos for our annual picnic and found them to be educational and very popular.

Puppy Pal and Kitty Kat Headbands

Precut triangle-shaped cat ears and headbands out of construction paper. Tape two ears to each headband. The children decorate them with furry fabric scraps. An adult uses Caran d'Ache Swedish Water Soluble Crayons to add whiskers and a pink dot on the child's nose. Also precut floppy ears and headbands from brown construction paper and tape two ears to each headband so they hang down over the child's ears. Decorate with furry fabric scraps, and add a black dot to the tips of the "puppies'" noses.

VIDEOS

See How They Grow PETS (Sony Wonder, 1995).

The Pet Forgetters Cure, with Jean Stapleton (MCA Records).

REFRESHMENTS

Provide animal crackers and Popsicles made by mixing vanilla yogurt and fruit juice. Pour the mixture into paper cups with Popsicle sticks, freeze, and peel away the cup before serving.

BOOKS

My Cats Nick and Nora, by Isabelle Harper (New York: Scholastic, 1995).

Pet Show, by Ezra Jacks Keats (New York: Macmillan, 1972).

The Little Duck, by Judy Dunn (New York: Random, 1976).

I Really Want A Dog, by Susan Breslow (New York: Dutton, 1990).

Fun in the Sun

This is an outdoor event that naturally requires a warm and sunny day. Invitations to the event can be made from the reproducible example (see page 75).

ACTIVITIES

Pool Party

Fill plastic swimming pools with a variety of objects. For example, place sand, sand toys, and seashells in one pool, and water and a collection of rubber ducks in another. Put toy boats and water colored with food coloring in a third. Have some pools that are filled only with water. Another possibility is to have bubbly, soapy water in a pool.

Sun Hats

Talk about sun safety, how important it is to protect ourselves from too much sun, and explain that a sun hat can provide us with shade. Precut the center out of 9-inch paper plates. The children decorate them with markers and wear them as sun visors.

Paper Fans
Cut 9-inch paper plates in half. Color with neon markers.

Beach Towels
Children and parents make designer beach towels on large sheets of butcher paper.

Rock People
Provide large, smooth, roundish rocks for the children to decorate. If you don't have such rocks in your area, get some from a nursery. Supply paint, pieces of costume jewelry, fabric scraps, yarn for hair, and white glue to attach wiggly eyes.

Rock Painting
Cover a working area with plenty of newspaper. The children collect rocks, lay them on the paper, and paint them with neon tempera paints. This is a favorite summertime activity.

ATTIRE Children should wear summer clothes, with a swimsuit underneath if swimming is desired.

ENTERTAINMENT The children play musical pools. Play music while the children dance around the outside of one of the pools filled only with water. When the music stops, they sit in the pool.

REFRESHMENTS Serve lemonade, watermelon slices, and little fish crackers.

BOOKS *It Looked Like Split Milk*, by Charles G. Shaw (New York: Harper, 1947).

One Summer Day, by Kim Lewis (Cambridge, MA: Candlewick, 1996).

One HOT Summer Day, by Nina Crews (New York: Greenwillow, 1995).

Joe's Pool, by Claire Henley (New York: Hyperion, 1994).

A Beach Day, by Douglas Florian (New York: Greenwillow, 1990).

My Bike, by Donna Jakob (New York: Hyperion, 1994).

Tool Time Party

Working with tools helps children develop coordination and large and small motor control. They also learn that they have the ability to make things themselves, and that it can be fun. Provide both toy and real tools. Invitations can be prepared from the reproducible example (see page 75).

ACTIVITIES

Matching
Trace real tools on a large sheet of tagboard paper. Write the name of each tool under the traced shape. Cover the paper with clear contact paper. Place an open toolbox containing the tools that were traced next to the paper. The children match the tools with the shapes by placing the correct tool on its shape and trying to identify it.

Woodworking
Set up a space for supervised woodworking. You will need a tough surface, sanding blocks, nails, and real child-sized hammers. Provide wood scraps or use inexpensive woodworking kits that are available from craft stores or from Hands On Work (612-293-8690, Ext 35). Safety goggles for children are available from ABC School Supply (1-800-669-4222).

What's Inside?
Remove the backs from a variety of machines, clocks, computers, and telephones so the children can look inside, rearrange the parts, and wonder how they work.

Plumber
Fill a basket with several kinds of plastic tubes and pipe fittings for the children to connect together. Purchase the parts from hardware or building supply stores. When the "plumbing systems" are completed, the children test them out in a large tub of water or in a water table.

Block Building
The children build structures using wooden blocks, or using cardboard blocks that are made to look like bricks.

VIDEO

Play the video *Lets Build a Playhouse* (Vermont Story Works Inc., 1995). This video shows parents and children how to design and build their own playhouse. It includes a building plan.

REFRESHMENTS   Serve ice cream cones.

BOOKS

My Very First Book of Tools, by Eric Carle (New York: Crowell, 1986).
The Toolbox, by Anne Rockwell (New York: Aladdin, 1990).
Ernie's Little Toolbox, by Annie Ingle (New York: Random, 1991).

REPRODUCIBLES

INVITATIONS
(following page 87)

Fall Events
Family Fun and Information Fair
Walk-a-Thon
Field Trips
Fall Ball
Peacemaker Gathering
Book Fair
Fantasy Photos
Dinosaur Dig
Veggie Soup Soirée
Sweet Dreams Jammy Party

Winter Events
Gifts from the Heart
Winter Getaway
Meet the Artist
Winter Frolic
Dad and Me
Wild Rumpus
Parent Makeovers
Gym Night /A.M. Aerobics
Purple Crayon Party

Spring Events
Arbor Day Celebration
Victorian Tea Party
Baby Shower
Alice in Wonderland
Birthday Bash
Garden Party
Nature Hikes
Teddy Bear Picnic
Green Eggs and Ham Brunch
Graduation Ceremony

Summer Events
Fish Festival
Insect Extravaganza
Pet Show
Fun in the Sun
Tool Time Party

Special Event Organizer

Title _____

Date _____

Time _____

Alternate Date _____

N O T E S

_____

_____

_____

_____

_____

_____

P E R S O N N E L

TITLE	RESPONSIBILITIES	NAME	PHONE (DAY/NIGHT)
Chairperson	Coordinate personnel		
Co-chair	Assist chairperson		
Public Relations	Press release, flyers, invitations, posters		
Decorations	Purchase, prepare, install		
Entertainment	Music, audio, video, live, rentals, books		
Food & Beverage	Purchasing, preparing, serving, leftovers		
Setup	Tables, chairs, activities, large muscle equipment		
Host or Hostess	Greet guests, collect any admission, registration		
Supervision	Oversee and replenish activities, child safety		
Announcer	Welcoming, introductions, door prizes, thank-yous, closing		
Celebrities	Costumes, greet, circulate, pass out information		
Takedown and Cleanup	Tables, chairs, decorations, activities, large muscle equipment		
Alternate Volunteers	Check in on day of event		
Follow-up	Thank sponsors, thank volunteers, gather feedback, attendance, amount raised		
Sponsors	Solicit donations, material contributions, speakers		

Activities and Materials List

PREREGISTRATION INFORMATION

Admission Fee: _____

Count: _____

TITLE	MATERIALS	NOTES
ACTIVITY 1.		
ACTIVITY 2.		
ACTIVITY 3.		
ACTIVITY 4.		
ACTIVITY 5.		
ACTIVITY 6.		
ACTIVITY 7.		
Attire		
Decorations		
Entertainment		
Food & Beverage		
Music		
Video		
Rentals		

Walk-a-Thon Sponsor Form

PARTICIPANT REGISTRATION INFORMATION

Parents' Names _____

Children's Names _____

Address _____

Phone Number _____

Number Participating _____

Total Pledged _____

Please collect money when it is pledged and bring the envelope and this form to the Walk-a-Thon.

WAIVER

In consideration of the furtherance of the purposes and objectives of _____

_____, and in consideration of your permitting me to participate in the

_____ Walk-a-Thon, on behalf of myself, heirs, and representatives, I

waive and release any and all rights and claims for damages, whatsoever they may be, especially

against the _____ Walk-a-Thon, its officers, and

committee members, any governmental unit, as well as any other person connected with the Walk-

a-Thon, for any and all injuries arising out of the Walk-a-Thon.

Signature of Participant(s) _____

"My hand will never hit or hurt another person."

To pledge, place your hand inside the box and trace the outline of your hand with a crayon, pen, pencil, or marker. Next, decorate your pledge in any way you wish. Then sign your name as a final commitment to your pledge. Post your pledge in a place which is important to you. Encourage your friends and family to take the pledge too.

I'm a Bookworm

Name

BOOK LIST

Book Title:

Read to me by:

I think this book . . .

Book Title:

Read to me by:

I think this book . . .

Book Title:

Read to me by:

I think this book . . .

Book Title:

Read to me by:

I think this book . . .

Book Title:

Read to me by:

I think this book . . .

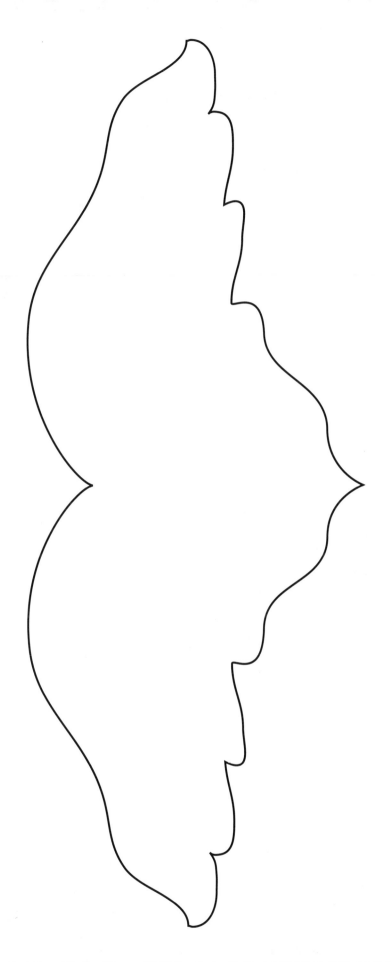

Angel Ornament Pattern

Meet the Artist

PHOTO OF THE CHILD

NAME _____

AGE _____

- -

TELL US ABOUT YOUR ARTWORK

Drawing, painting, coloring, and playing with playdough are fun because

_____

_____

_____

_____

_____

_____

_____

_____

_____

"Real People" Paper Doll

"Real People" Paper Doll

Handprints

My little feet could hardly walk,
My tiny mouth could barely talk.

Remember me when I was small,
Before my teeth or growing tall?

The first 'mama,' the first 'bye-bye,'
If you would go, I'd cry and cry.

I was so precious, you told me so,
That was how many years ago?

Please keep my handprints on the wall,
To remind us both, when I was small.

Yearbook

Certificate of Attendance

for the year _____

is presented to

_____

Parents and Child Together

My Family

_____
_____
_____

My Teachers

_____
_____

For more information, please call: ....

WHEN: ....

WHERE: ....

WHO: ....

Come to Our Family Fun and Information Fair!

ATTENTION

ALL FUN SEEKERS

For information, please call:
....

WHEN:
....

WHERE:
....

WHO:
....

Everyone is Welcome!

FRESH AIR + EXERCISE +
FRIENDS +
THE GREAT OUTDOORS +
RAISING MONEY FOR
A GOOD CAUSE +
GREAT THINGS TO EAT AND
DRINK = BIG FUN

Walking has never been this much fun.

Well, the part about being invited is true, but the part about our destination was a little mixed up. We are actually going to

We are going on a field trip to an island in the Pacific Ocean. You are not going to believe this, but you are invited!!

our Fall Ball.
of the season at
the sights and smells
Come and celebrate

FALL!

©1997. Let's Party!
Redleaf Press, 450 N. Syndicate, St. Paul, MN 55104-4125
1-800-423-8309

FOR A LIMITED
TIME ONLY . . .

For more information, please call:

WHEN:

WHERE:

WHO:

*Come to our
peace
gathering!*

*Make a
difference in
the world . . .*

Come to Our Book Fair!

GET SMART!

NOW JUST STAY LIKE THAT
UNTIL IT'S TIME FOR OUR
PHOTO FANTASY PARTY!

WHAT:
An opportunity not to be missed. Bring your camera and plenty of film to take pictures of your child in a variety of fantasy settings. If you don't have a camera, pictures of your child can be purchased for a minimal fee. Now hold that smile, and we'll see you there!

WHO:
....

WHERE:
....

WHEN:
....

For more information, please call:
....

SAY CHEESE PLEASE!

SMILE . . . SAY, "CHEESE."
THAT'S IT . . . SAY, "HAWAII."
SMILE . . . HOLD THAT POSE.

For more information, please call:
....

WHEN:
....

WHERE:
....

WHO:
....

THE DINO DIG
PARTY!

YABA-DABA-DOO
You are
invited to . . .

Please stop by
our Soup Soirée
(*swah-ray*)
We'll all have
soup while the
children play!

WHO: ....

WHERE: ....

WHEN: ....

WHAT TO BRING:
Please donate a fresh vegetable on the day before the event. Thank-you!

For more information, please call: ....

Awesome carrots, broccoli,
and tomatoes. Luscious
zucchini, leeks, and
potatoes. Celery, peas,
eggplant, and greens,
all the things that
keep us keen.

WHO:

WHERE:

WHEN:

WHAT TO WEAR: Pajamas

For more information, please call:

(FAVORITE BEDTIME TOYS CAN COME TOO!)

COME TO OUR
SWEET DREAMS
JAMMY PARTY!

SLEEP TIGHT,
DON'T LET THE
BEDBUGS BITE

For more information, please call:
....

WHEN:
....

WHERE:
....

WHO:
....

Say "I Care" in a way that department stores cannot. At our *Gifts from the Heart* party we will provide all of the materials necessary for you and your children to make gifts that money can't buy.

Gifts from the Heart...

WINTER BREAK

Join us for a winter getaway!

WHO: ....

WHERE: ....

WHEN: ....

WHAT TO WEAR: Tropical Togs (beneath warm clothes) ....

For more information, please call: ....

Come and
"MEET THE
ARTIST"
right here at
home!

Don't go to
PARIS
Forget about
ROME

WINTER FROLIC

A CELEBRATION OF WINTER!

WHO:

WHERE:

WHEN:

For more information, please call:

Jack Frost promises not to bite your nose and cordially invites you to attend...

IF DAD CAN'T COME,
IT'S NOT THE END,
INVITE YOUR GRANDPA,
UNCLE, OR A FRIEND!

©1997. Let's Party!
Redleaf Press, 450 N. Syndicate, St. Paul, MN 55104-4125
1-800-423-8309

A SPECIAL DAY FOR
DAD AND ME

Do your children ever
feel like pounding their
chests and swinging
from the trees?

Then
bring them
to the
WILD
RUMPUS!

WHO: ....

WHERE: ....

WHEN: ....

WHAT TO WEAR: Something wild and crazy!

For more information, please call:

Come to our special
event and speak with
experts in making people
look and feel good. You
could also be the winner
of a fabulous parent
makeover!

CHILD CARE WILL BE AVAILABLE ON A LIMITED BASIS.

WHO:
....

WHERE:
....

WHEN:
....

For more information, please call:
....

IF YOUR ANSWER TO BOTH OF
THESE QUESTIONS IS "b"
YOU QUALIFY FOR OUR
SPECIAL GYM EVENT.

IF EITHER ANSWER WAS "a"
YOU SUPER-QUALIFY FOR THE
EVENT.

DO YOU WANT TO BE
☐ *a.* A couch potato?
☐ *b.* A bundle of energy?

WOULD YOU RATHER
☐ *a.* Reach for a candy bar?
☐ *b.* Reach for the stars?

Purple Crayon Party

Purple paint
and purple play,
please join us
for purple day!

WHO: ....

WHERE: ....

WHEN: ....

WHAT TO WEAR: Purple, of course! ....

For more information, please call: ....

Come to our
Arbor Day
celebration!

WHO: ....

WHERE: ....

WHEN: ....

For more information, please call: ....

AN ARBOR DAY TREE
Dear little tree that we plant today,
What will you be when we're old and gray?
The savings bank of the squirrel and mouse,
For the robin and wren an apartment house.
The dressing room of the butterfly's ball,
The locust's and katydid's concert hall.
The school boy's ladder in pleasant June,
The school girl's tent in the July noon.
And my leaves shall whisper right merrily,
A tale of children who planted me.

—AUTHOR UNKNOWN

*This
Victorian Tea
is Just
for You!*

*Please
and
Thank You,
Tootle-Loo!*

YOU'RE INVITED
TO OUR BABY
SHOWER!

GOO-GOO, GA-GA . . .

IS THERE A BABY IN THE HOUSE?

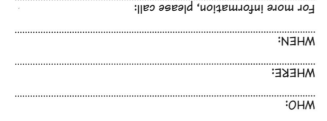

Come to our
ALICE IN
WONDERLAND
PARTY!

WHO: ....

WHERE: ....

WHEN: ....

For more information, please call:
....

"Oh Dear, Oh Dear.
Don't be late!"

——————————

is a very important
date!

IT'S A
BIRTHDAY
BASH AND
YOU ARE
INVITED!

WE ARE CELEBRATING 365 BIRTHDAYS!

Happy Birthday

Come to our
garden party,
and we will let
you know!

How does your garden grow?

JOIN OTHER
NATURE LOVERS
FOR A WALK IN
THE WOODS.

TAKE A
HIKE!

IT WOULD BE
UNBEARABLE
WITHOUT YOU!!

COME TO OUR
TEDDY BEAR
PICNIC!

Try them…
You may
become a fan!
Come to our Green
Eggs and Ham
brunch!

WHO: ....

WHERE: ....

WHEN: ....

WHAT TO BRING: ....

For more information, please call:
....

You do not like green eggs and ham?

For more information, please call: ....

WHEN: ....

WHERE: ....

WHO: ....

We've played hard
and learned a ton,
You're invited to
join the fun!

The Class of

—————

*Requests the Honor
Of Your Presence
At Our
Graduation Ceremony*

DO YOU LIKE TO
TELL ABOUT THE
ONE THAT GOT
AWAY?

THEN BE SURE
TO COME TO
OUR FISH
FESTIVAL DAY!

WHO: ....

WHERE: ....

WHEN: ....

For more information, please call:
....

Come to Our Insect Extravaganza!

WE'RE GOING TO BUG YOU!

For more information, please call:

WHEN:

WHERE:

WHO:

SHOW!
AT OUR PET
ANIMALS
LEARN ABOUT

MEOW,
BOW-WOW

THERE'S SO MUCH TO KNOW

You are invited to our
Fun in the
Sun party!

WHO:

WHERE:

WHEN:

WHAT TO WEAR: Cool clothes, swimsuits

For more information, please call:

Grab a beach towel,
head for the sun!
Put on your shades,
we're gonna have fun!

Tool Time!
Please come to our
Tool Time party.

WHAT TIME IS IT?